Ranks and Challenges for Psychological Skills: Student Manual

Joseph Strayhorn, Jr.

Psychological Skills Press

Psychological Skills Press

Wexford, PA

www.psychologicalskills.org

author's email: joestrayhorn@gmail.com

The cover photo is the Nobel Peace Prize medal that was given to Rigoberta Menchú and is protected in the Templo Mayor Museum in Mexico City. This creative work was taken by Protoplasma Kid and uploaded under a Creative Commons license.

ISBN: 978-1-931773-25-6

Table of Contents

What This Book Is For

1. Students learn lots of skills: playing a musical instrument, swimming, playing a sport, doing math. This book has to do with psychological skills. These are the skills useful in reaching two big goals: 1) to lead a happy life, and 2) to help other people to lead happy lives. Productivity, joyousness, kindness, and others are examples of psychological skills.

Which of the following two do you think is more likely to be called a psychological skill?

A. The skill of staying calm when things don't go your way.
or
B. Skill in playing football.

2. One important way of helping yourself get better at skills is called monitoring. Monitoring means that you measure your skill and see how you are progressing. It is possible to read a lot about skills but not get better at them. The way to really know whether you have mastered a skill is to test yourself. Track runners time themselves. Weightlifters see how much they can lift. Musicians see how good their music sounds to careful

listeners. Video games usually monitor how well you are doing and let you "level up" as you get more skilled.

What's the point of this section?

A. To get better at skills, work hard and read a lot about how to get better.
or
B. When you're working at skills, it's good to test yourself to monitor how skilled you are.

3. There are at least two reasons to monitor yourself. First, if you get evidence that you are improving, this is a reason to feel good. Good feelings about progress reward your efforts and make it easier to make more progress. Second, if you test yourself and discover something you don't know how to do yet, then you can put it on your to do list, or you can get busy and learn and practice it right on the spot.
Either way, you have reason to feel good! You celebrate the things you already know, and you celebrate that you are learning!

What's a summary of this unit?

A. Monitoring yourself helps you feel good about what you've learned and figure out what you need to learn.
or

B. Some people are afraid to test themselves because they are afraid of criticism or failure or being laughed at.

4. Here's another reason to monitor your progress. If you have a tutor or teacher, then that person can feel good also at seeing how much progress you have made. You have the opportunity to make someone else happy by showing how much you have learned.

In this unit the author appears to believe that at least some of the time,

A. Students want to make their teachers happy.
or
B. Students have friends who are more fun to be with if they are better at psychological skills.

5. Several skill training programs use ranks and challenges. In martial arts, people get tested to go from one color belt to another. In Boy Scouts, people earn ranks that reflect how much they have learned. In Red Cross swimming instruction, people demonstrate their skills in a series of levels. Each level has a set of requirements to pass—some skills that you demonstrate that you've learned.

All of these programs, as well as ours, start with easier challenges and work the way up to harder ones. Having a system that works the way up from easier to harder is another advantage of a system of ranks and challenges.

What's an example of starting with easier challenges and working up to harder ones?

A. Starting out playing songs on the piano like "Twinkle Twinkle Little Star," and working your way up to very challenging songs like "Maple Leaf Rag."
or
B. Starting out wearing small shoes, and wearing bigger ones the more you grow?

6. Working on ranks and challenges is one way of doing something called "mastery learning." With mastery learning, you start with easier challenges, and work your way up. You keep working until you've mastered the skill you're working on. There's no penalty if you try a certain challenge and can't do it. You don't get a bad grade. You just keep working and try again later. There's no worry about failure -- the only question is how long it takes you to succeed.

Which of the following is a mastery learning program?

A. A teacher teaches a course, that lasts 3 months; at the end of that time if you pass a test, you have passed the course. Otherwise you fail.
or

B. A teacher has skills arranged in order of difficulty. You keep working on any skill until you've gotten good at it. If you test yourself and find you aren't good at it yet, you just keep working until you are good at it.

7. This book goes with a program for learning psychological skills. Students in this program can read lots of books. The skills that are tested in the Ranks and Challenges are explained in these books. Two of the very important books are *Programmed Readings for Psychological Skills* and *A Programmed Course in Psychological Skills Exercises*. This book is a review book (along with some new ideas that will be included in the next editions of the books I just named!) There is one chapter for each level in the Ranks and Challenges program. It's good to read the chapter just before you test yourself for a level, to bring to mind what you will do when you try to pass that level.

What's the point of this unit?

A. This book helps you to be ready to pass the various levels in our Ranks and Challenges for Psychological Skills.

or

B. The skills that are tested in the various levels have been chosen very carefully to be skills that help people to be happy and make others happy.

8. Here are the steps that you and your tutor go through in passing a level.

First, you learn about the skills by reading other books in this series, such as Programmed Readings or the Exercises book.

Second, you and your tutor practice doing exercises.

Third, you read the chapter in this book that corresponds to the level you are testing for. (You start with level 1 and go in order.)

Fourth, you and your tutor practice doing the challenges for that level. You keep going until your tutor thinks you can do every one of the challenges really well.

Fifth, your tutor records one or more sessions where you do the challenges.

Sixth, someone else in our organization listens to that recording to see if you passed.

Seventh, if you did, you celebrate! You include your tutor and your family in the celebration. If you did not pass yet, you don't worry! You just keep working until you do pass!

Eighth, you keep practicing the skills you've learned, because: you're not just learning them to pass a rank; you're learning them because they are very useful!

What's a point that this unit made?

A. You keep studying and practicing until you can do all the challenges for a certain rank well. Then you record yourself doing them. Someone else listens to the recording. You celebrate each rank that you pass!
or
B. If your tutor doesn't know what a good performance on a certain challenge should sound like, this may be an opportunity for the tutor to learn that.

Level 1

1.1. Two big goals

9. Here's the first requirement for Level 1:

Tell the two big goals that people use psychological skills to achieve. (These are the two big goals of OPT and what some people consider the two central goals of life.)

Here's the answer: the two big goals are that 1) you have a happy life, and 2) you help others to have a happy life. In other words, you do things that make yourself and others happier. Put another way: kindness to yourself, and kindness to other people.

What's another way of saying the two big goals?

A. Caring for self, and caring for others.
or
B. Making enough money and defeating those who compete with you.

10. Some people have said that it's not advisable to try to be happy, but that happiness comes only from working toward other goals. But I think that when you make decisions, it is important to take your own happiness into account. Suppose I am fixing supper. Let's imagine that I love green peas and I hate Lima

beans. Which should I pick? The two are about equally healthy, so I pick the one I like! Suppose I think I would enjoy being a doctor and would not like being an engineer. Which should I pick? Both of them do good for people -- why not do the one I think I would enjoy more? Or suppose I'm wanting to get married: should I ask someone I really like to be with, or someone that I very much dislike? In all these choices, the sensible thing to do, of course, is to make the choice that will make me happier!

What's the point of this section?

A. If you are too selfish and think only about what's best for you, that's not the way to be happy.
or
B. When we make choices, it's reasonable to take into account what we think will make us happy in the long run.

11. A couple of thousand years ago, a wise person named Hillel said, "“If I am not for myself, who will be for me? If I am only for myself, what am I?" Do you see that Hillel used different words to refer to the two big goals of kindness to self and kindness to others?

Long before that, other smart people came up with the saying, "Love your neighbor as yourself." This is still another way of saying that we should be kind to other people as well as to ourselves.

What is a conclusion that follows from this unit?

A. The author of this book certainly does not claim to be the first one to think up the two big goals of kindness to self and kindness to others.
or
B. So much competition in sports, business, and academics tends to make people unaware that they can increase their own happiness by increasing other people's happiness.

1.2. Listing 16 skills

12. Here's the next requirement for Level 1.
Listen to the song, "What are the Qualities," at least once. (It's at optskills.org/songs.) Be able to list all the 16 psychological skills, in order, after being given a brief phrase that reminds you of each of them.

These are the skills that help us to achieve the two big goals. People who are good at these skills have a much better chance to be happier themselves and to make other people happy.

Here are the words to the song:

What are the qualities that make life better? What makes people good?

What lets people live in happiness and peace, and brother- and sister-hood?

Productivity, joyousness, kindness, honesty, fortitude;
Good decisions made every day, nonviolence and not being rude. (not being rude = respectful talk)

Friendship-building, self-discipline, loyalty, conservation and self-care;
Compliance and positive fantasy rehearsal and courage, if you dare.

There are really 17 skills if you count individual decisions and joint decisions as two separate skills. Joint decisions include conflict-resolution.

You can download the song if you want, from optskills.org/songs. It's called "What are the Qualities" in the "Spirit of Nonviolence" section.

What are the first five skills on the list, in order?

A. Productivity, joyousness, kindness, honesty, fortitude
or
B. Positive fantasy rehearsal, loyalty, conservation, compliance, self-care?

13. If you want a way of remembering the skills, other than the song, think about the following sentence:

Please, just keep her from getting nine rattlesnakes,
For several little children shall calmly play closeby.

The first letter of each of the words in these sentences gives the first letter of the sixteen skills. You might be able to think of a better sentence, or pair of sentences, with the letters PJKHFGNR, FSLCSCPC. Can you look at the letters and name the skill that starts with each letter?

Why is it good to have this list memorized? Because these are the types of behaviors that you will want to celebrate and feel good about. These are the types of good behaviors that you want to remember lots of positive examples of. In every situation you face, you have the opportunity to do a good example of at least one of these. These are key to leading a life that brings happiness to you and the people around you.

Why does the author talk about rattlesnakes and playing children?

A. Because he doesn't want you to get pet rattlesnakes if children are around, because the children could get bitten as they play calmly closeby.
or
B. Because the sentences give clues that can help you remember the 16 skills.

14. Here's an example of the types of phrases that are used by the tester to remind you of the 16 skills, in order. Practice until they clue you to remember the skills, even without looking at the words. I suggest that the tutor read out these phrases, quickly, and the student say the names of the skills. I recommend doing this not just once, but several times.

1. Getting things accomplished by being industrious.
2. Taking pleasure in the good things that happen.
3. Being nice to someone else.
4. Telling the truth.
5. Handling it when unwanted things happen.
6. Thinking carefully about what to do.
7. Not hitting, kicking, shooting, or stabbing.
8. Speaking in a civil way to others, without needlessly insulting them.
9. Getting to know and like other people.
10. Being tough and strong enough to choose an action that helps achieve a goal, even when it isn't fun.
11. Making good choices about whom to stick up for and support.
12. Being thrifty.
13. Making choices that keep you and others healthy.
14. Obeying rules unless they are bad rules.
15. Practicing in imagination doing good things.
16. Doing the best choice, even when it's scary or aversive.

The main purpose of doing this is

A. To work toward being able to remember all the skills even without the prompts, and to be very familiar with what they are.
or
B. To pick up some new vocabulary words that will help you on tests of vocabulary.

15. Now let's do the same thing again, only with a different list of reminders.

1. Getting work done.
2. Experiencing happiness whenever there's a reason to.
3. Helping someone else.
4. Having integrity and not deceiving people.
5. Putting up with not getting your way.
6. Trying to work things out well when two people need to choose what to do about something.
7. Working for peace.
8. Being polite.
9. Making and strengthening good relationships.
10. Being able to make yourself do what's best, even when tempted to do other things.
11. Keeping your commitments to other people.
12. Helping out the planet by not being wasteful.
13. Doing things safely.

14. Doing what parents or teachers tell you, unless they have made a mistake and are telling you to do something wrong.
15. Avoiding entertaining yourself by violent images.
16. Not letting unrealistic fear or aversions get in the way of doing what's best.

Why do you think the author wants you to use certain particular words for these, rather than just making up a word or phrase?

A. Because he believes he's made up words that are better than those anyone else could make up.
or
B. Because he wants the names of the psychological skills to come "automatically," so that you don't have to waste energy searching for the right word or phrase.

16. Now, rather than just reading this, please practice naming the 16 skills and principles. Below is a very brief reminder for each. Please look at each of these and say the official word for the skill.

1. Working
2. Enjoying
3. Helping
4. Truth
5. Frustration-tolerance (A frustration is something happening that you don't like.)

6. Choosing
7. No hurting
8. Courtesy
9. Socializing
10. Being tough
11. Commitments
12. Saving
13. Healthiness
14. Obeying
15. Imagining
16. Bravery

1.3. Identifying skills for stories

17. Here's the next requirement for Level 1:

Listen to three stories and tell what skill the story models.

If you've read the skills stories in Programmed Readings for Psychological Skills, you are very familiar with this sort of exercise.

Let's drill just a little bit on the list of psychological skills. Take a look at the following four story plots. Then match each of them with one of the psychological skills.

1. Someone dislikes what someone else has done, but they speak politely to the person.

2. Someone made a mistake, but does not try to hide it, and speaks openly about it.
3. Someone considers spending money on entertainment, but decides to save the money instead.
4. Someone is nervous and worried about failing at a job, but shows up at the job and tries their hardest anyway.

Here are the four skills for you to match them to:

A. Honesty
B. Courage
C. Respectful talk
D. Conservation

Please figure out which letter goes with each number.

18. Let's do the same thing with four more skills.

1. Someone at an emergency room helps an injured person, and while doing so, speaks in a very nice way to that person.
2. Someone passes up a bunch of potato chip and pop, and has healthier food that doesn't taste quite as good.
3. Someone reads and talks to people a lot, to find out information that will help the person choose what career to go into.

4. Someone applies for a job, and is turned down. But the person doesn't let bad feelings about this get them down, and handles the disappointment well.

Here are the skills to match them to.

A. Fortitude
B. Kindness
C. Good individual decisions
D. Self-discipline

19. Now let's do it for four more skills.

1. Someone wakes up and can't get back to sleep. The person cleans up the kitchen and organizes the things around their desk, and then goes back to bed.
2. Someone focuses as much as possible on what someone else is saying, using reflections, facilitations, follow-up questions, and positive feedback to be a good listener in the conversation.
3. Someone sticks up for an old friend, remembering when the friend did kind things for them.
4. Someone wears a mask during a pandemic, to look after their own health as well as that of others.

Here are the skills to match to them:

A. Loyalty
B. Friendship-building

C. Self-care
D. Productivity

20. Last round of this exercise! This time match 5 skills to 5 story plots.

1. Someone has a disagreement, but they talk it out in a calm and reasonable way.
2. Someone follows the rules about paying taxes, even though they wish they didn't have to.
3. Someone avoids playing a really violent video game because they don't want to practice not caring whether people are hurt, even when the people are just imaginary.
4. Someone reads history and realizes how much better things are now than they were in the past, and the person feels really good to think about this.
5. When there is an election, someone works hard to try to get a candidate elected who is opposed to starting wars.

And here are the skills:

A. Compliance
B. Joyousness
C. Nonviolence
D. Positive fantasy rehearsal
E. Good joint decisions or conflict resolution

21. When you do the test, you probably will not be given two choices for the stories. You will have to just come up with the words on your own. This won't be hard if you're familiar with the words for the 16 skills and principles. Some of the stories may have more than one correct answer. It's difficult to make up something good that someone has done that is an example of only one of the 16 skills.

What did the author just say about the requirement you've just been reading about?

A. You'll hear a story, plus two skills, and pick which one the story gives an example of.
or
B. You'll hear stories and will be asked to tell what skill each story gives an example of, without being given two choices.

22. Let's practice this. Here's a little skill story.

Yan went to visit some people. The people were all smoking a certain drug, and they invited Yan to join them. But Yan had read good scientific studies showing that this drug sometimes makes people get very scared about nothing; it sometimes takes away people's motivation to accomplish things; it also seems to make people less smart the more they use it. So Yan said no, and Yan decided to go back home before long.

Which of the 16 skills do you think this story illustrates?

1.4. Celebrations exercise

23. The fourth requirement for level 1 is to be able to do the celebrations exercise.

Tell at least 3 things you have done that are positive examples of a psychological skill, and identify which skill(s) each is an example of. (This is the celebrations exercise.)

Here's an example of a celebration:

"Today I saw on the sidewalk an earthworm who was on the sidewalk as it got hotter and dryer. I picked it up and put it over into the dirt where it wouldn't dry out and die. That was a little act of kindness."

Here's another example:

"Today I got the urge to buy a really expensive video game. But I decided instead to save my money. That was conservation and self-discipline."

Here's another example:

"Today I sang some songs with my sister, harmonizing together. We really had fun! It was friendship-building and joyousness!"

Do you think the following sentence is true, or false? Everything that someone can do that is wise or good can be used in the celebrations exercise.

A. True,
or
B. False?

24. Why do we do the celebrations exercise? There are two reasons. Each time you remember something good that you've done and feel good about it, you are rewarding yourself for doing it, and making it more likely you'll do something like that again. Second, each time you feel good about something you've done, you make yourself a little happier.

What's a summary of this text unit?

A. When you do the celebrations exercise, you can think of anything good that you have done in your whole life.
or
B. Doing the celebrations exercise helps you to 1) do wise or good things more often, and 2) to be happier from feeling good about your own choices.

1.5. Skills stories exercise

25. The fifth requirement for level 1 is the skills stories exercise.
Make up and tell 2 stories where a character gives positive models of psychological skill, and identify which skill(s) each is an example of.

Here's an example of a skills story:

One time Sula was at a party. Someone named Ginto was dared to make a speech that would be as offensive to as many groups as possible; Ginto got up and acted really stupid and said a lot of things that Ginto didn't mean. Sula happened to have a phone video on, and made a video of Ginto. Later, Sula got the urge to post the video on social media. But Sula thought about the pros and cons, and figured that this might be really embarrassing for Ginto and maybe get Ginto into a lot of trouble. So Sula deleted the video instead of posting it. But Sula told Ginto that Ginto should watch out in the future in case someone else didn't make the same judgment.

A. Good decisions and kindness,
or
B. Positive fantasy rehearsal and productivity?

26. Here's another example of a skills story:

Someone was scuba diving in the ocean. The person found an underwater cave that looked really beautiful. The person got the urge to go into the cave and look around, but they noticed that there was a current going into the cave. The person thought, "What if the current would get stronger so that I couldn't get out once I got in?" So the person decided to stay out of the cave.

A. honesty and conservation,
or
B. self-care and good decisions.

27. Why is the skills stories exercise something good to do? Because each time you do it, you are using positive fantasy rehearsal. You are practicing doing something good, in your imagination, and that will probably help you do more of whatever skill you're imagining, in real life.

What's a summary of this?

A. The skills stories exercise lets us use positive fantasy rehearsal to practice all the psychological skills.
or
B. When you feel good about something good that happens, that's joyousness; when you are reasonable when something bad happens, that's fortitude. So almost every good or bad thing that happens lets us practice a psychological skill.

1.6. Divergent thinking exercise

28. The sixth requirement for Level 1 is to do the divergent thinking exercise:

Given a question that can have many answers, take turns with someone to generate a total of at least 10 different answers (where you think of at least 5 of them).

The divergent thinking exercise is meant to exercise your creativity, your ability to think of lots of different possibilities for a question you are pondering. It prepares you for thinking of lots of options for solving problems, and lots of pros and cons when you're considering options.

Here's an example of the divergent thinking exercise.

The question is: Someone left their house at 3 a.m., when it was very dark out. Why did the person do that?

Below are some possible answers. I recommend that the tutor and student take turns reading them.

1. The person had a sick family member, and the person had to take the family member to the hospital.

2. The person worked outside during a very hot summer, and the people at the work site agreed to start very early in the morning to escape the heat.
3. The person woke up and couldn't get back to sleep, and decided to go outside for a walk.
4. The person had an appointment in another town that they had to drive to, and they got started early to arrive on time.
5. The person worked at a job that had shifts, and the person's shift started at 330 am.
6. The person caught a bat inside their house and went outside to turn the bat loose.
7. The person woke up and realized their wallet was lost, and went out to look for it.
8. The person wanted to look at the stars.
9. The person's house had caught fire.
10. The person heard a lot of people making a lot of noise and went out to ask them to be quieter.

Why do you think the author recommended taking turns reading the ideas for the divergent thinking exercise?

A. Because they take turns in just the same way when they are actually doing the exercise and thinking up the ideas themselves.
or
B. Because then nobody's voice gets too tired from having to talk for too long.

1.7. Getting to know you questions

29. The seventh requirement is:

Answer one question for each of the following three "getting to know you" exercises: would you rather, sentence completion, questions for getting to know someone.

All you do for this is to answer the questions, and say whatever you want about why you answered that way. Here's what it might sound like.

Would you rather:

Tutor: Would you rather be the fastest runner in your state, or the best computer programmer in your state?

Student: I think that I'd rather be the best computer programmer, because I could probably earn lots of money and I probably could do some things that would help people.

Sentence completion:

Tutor: I felt proud when ______.

Student: I felt proud of my sister when she graduated from high school.

Questions for getting to know someone:

Tutor: Please say anything you want about pain.

Student: One time I hurt my knee and had to not run or walk very much for a while, and I didn't like that at all. I was really glad when it got well, and I appreciate that I'm not in pain any more.

What is the purpose of the would you rather, sentence completion, and questions for getting to know someone exercises?

A. To practice getting the right answers to the questions that are asked in these exercises.
or
B. To let people practice sharing with each other their thoughts and feelings, and to get conversations started.

30. Why are these exercises good to do? Because if you can enjoy telling other people about your thoughts and experiences, and enjoy hearing about their thoughts and experiences, you have a way of making yourself and others happy that will last throughout your life!

What's a summary of this?

A. The author thinks that people who enjoy chatting with each other have a skill that helps out enormously in being happy and making each other happy.
or
B. If you go for an interview, it's good to be used to talking about yourself.

1.8. Guess the feelings exercise

31. The last requirement for level 1 is like the Guess the Feelings exercise.
Given two vignettes and what the person thought in the situation, pick, among choices, what the person probably was feeling in the situation.

For the Guess the Feelings exercise, people make up situations where it would be very believable for people to feel either of at least two very different feelings. But when you hear the clue of what the person thought to themselves, then it should become clear which of the feelings is correct.

There are three purposes of the Guess the Feelings exercise: 1) to get very familiar with "feeling words," so that we can use them in thinking about life, and 2) to recognize how much our feelings depend on what we say to ourselves, and 3) that the two people doing it with each other get to know each other better and maybe feel closer to each other.

In the Guess the Feelings Exercise, what's the important clue that is meant to give away how the person felt?

A. Telling what the person said to themselves about the situation they were in.
or
B. Telling what letter the feeling begins with.

32. Lots of times when people have each other guess things, the goal is to stump the other person -- there's a competition. With all the guessing games we do, that's not the purpose. It's a cooperative activity and not a competition. In fact, after you give the clue telling what the person was thinking, the person guessing should almost always be able to guess the right answer.

What's a summary of this?

A. Feeling words are useful, because in one word they can summarize a lot of important stuff going on in ourselves.
or
B. The Guess the Feelings activity is one where you actually want your partner to get the right answer, not to stump them.

33. Here are a bunch of words that describe feelings, that can be used in the Guess the Feelings exercise. If two people are reading this list aloud, I recommend that you take turns, shifting to the other reader with each feeling word.

List of Feeling Words

Usually pleasant feelings: accepted, appreciative, amused, awed, attracted, calm, cheerful, compassionate, curious, close, confident, contented, elated, excited, free, friendly, fun, glad, glowing, grateful, happy, hopeful, interested, jolly, joyful, lighthearted, liking, love, moved, playful, pleasant, pleased, proud, relaxed, relieved, satisfied, self-assured, serene, silly, slaphappy, sympathetic, tenderness, thankful, tickled, wonder

Usually unpleasant feelings: afraid, angry, annoyed, ashamed, bitter, bored, bothered, burdened, disdainful, drained, brokenhearted, confused, impatient, disappointed, disgusted, displeased, disturbed, embarrassed, energized, envious, startled, fearful, frazzled, frightened, frustrated, guilty, harried, hate, hopeless, horrified, hurt, impatient, irritated, jealous, lonely, low, mad, mortified, pain, rage, regret, resentment, sad, scared, self-critical, shocked, terrified, threatened, tormented, troubled, uncomfortable, uneasy, unfriendly, unpleasant, upset, worried

Could be pleasant or unpleasant: amazed, astonished, bewildered, concerned, flabbergasted, indifferent, excited, pity, worn out, suspicious, stirred.

If someone really dislikes what someone else has done, and strongly disapproves, it would be more likely that the person feels

A. disdainful,
or
B. appreciative?

34. Here's an example of the Guess the Feelings exercise. A person is set to go on a picnic. But there's a thunderstorm, and the picnic is canceled. Did the person feel relieved, or disappointed? Before the clue, someone could take a random guess: "Let's see: I'll guess that the person was disappointed, because they were looking forward to having a good time." But then here's the clue: the person said to themselves, "Thank goodness. I never know what to say to those people, and I don't think they like me at all. I don't know why I ever said I'd go on that picnic in the first place."

Now the guesser knows the answer: the person felt:

A. relieved,
or
B. disappointed?

35. Here's a second example. A person gets back from taking a run, and notices that the time is 3:30 pm. Does the person feel proud, or very upset? If the guesser takes a random guess at this stage, it might go like this: "I'm going to guess the person is very upset, because they realize they had an appointment that started at 3 o'clock, and they missed it." But then here's the clue: the person thought, "Yay! I ran that distance faster than I ever have before! I'm getting in better and better shape!"

Now the guesser knows the answer: the person felt:

A. very upset,
or
B. proud.

36. All you have to do to meet the requirement is listen to a little story, get the clue of what the person thought, and choose correctly between two feelings. But if you want, and you are more familiar with this exercise, you can do the exercise a little more thoroughly. You can make up a story yourself, tell the other, name two plausible feelings, let the other take a random guess, then tell the person what the person said to themselves, and then tell the correct feeling.

A summary of this is that

A. Just guessing the feeling meets the requirement; if you want to go the extra mile and make up a story yourself, give two feelings, and make up the self-talk that gives away the answer, you are welcome to do so!
or
B. If there are some of the feeling words whose meanings you are not sure of, it's recommended that you use a dictionary, either one made of paper or one on the Internet, to check out how these feeling words are defined.

37. When you finish Level 1 of the ranks and challenges, you have reason to celebrate! Just having in mind the two big goals of happiness for self and happiness of others is an accomplishment in itself. Being very familiar with a bunch of the skills that accomplish those goals is celebration-worthy. Being able to remember, and make up, positive examples of those skills are activities that will help you for the rest of your life, if you do them.

The divergent thinking exercise prepares you for both brainstorming options and thinking of pros and cons when you are making decisions. The getting to know each other exercises are meant to give fun experience in chatting with someone else, and if you can enjoy that, you'll have a source of happiness throughout life. And the guess the feelings exercise, introduces you to how your feelings depend on your self-talk, which is a very important idea!

The author is saying that

A. The skills tested in Level 1 are very useful for anyone to know.
or
B. It's good to practice relaxing, because this is a very important skill that falls within the skill of self-care.

Level 2

2.1. Reflections exercise

38. Here's the first requirement for Level 2:

Let someone read to you the thoughts and utterances of an imaginary person. Each time the person stops talking, do a reflection of what the person said. It's fine to use the prompts for reflections while doing this. (This is the reflections exercise.)

Doing reflections is a way to be a good listener. You make sure you understand what the other person has said, by saying it back in different words. You let the other person know that you understand, and this can feel good to the other person. If you misunderstand, you give the other person a chance to correct your misunderstanding. Reflections help people to communicate better.

What's a summary?

A. Saying back what you understood someone to say helps you to make sure you got the message correctly; it also can feel good to the other person to know that you understood.
or

B. In addition to reflections, good listeners tend to use facilitations, follow-up questions, and positive feedback.

39. The reflections exercise is also a good exercise in concentration and focus. In order to reflect correctly, you have to really tune in to what the other person is saying. Lots of people don't realize how much their minds have gone elsewhere when someone else is talking, until they try to reflect.

What other benefit of doing the reflections exercise does this section talk about?

A. Practicing patience.
or
B. Practicing concentration.

40. If you begin a sentence with one of these seven prompts, you are probably using a reflection.

1. So you're saying ________________?
2. What I hear you saying is ________________.
3. In other words, ______________?
4. So if I understand you right, ______________?
5. It sounds like ________________.
6. Are you saying that ______________?
7. You're saying that _____________?

Level 2

To do requirement 1, listen as your tutor reads what someone says, and each time they stop talking, do a reflection. Try to do as "good" a reflection as possible.

What does requirement 1 consist of?

A. Doing a reflection each time the other person stops talking or reading.
or
B. Talking yourself and letting the other person do a reflection each time you stop.

41. Here's a way to practice doing the reflections exercise. One person -- the tutor, for example -- reads the part of the "talker" in a sample dialogue. The other -- the student, for example -- reads the part of the "listener." There are no A or B questions for the next few text units. Let the tutor play the part of the talker, and the student play the part of the listener. Here is the first sample dialogue.

Dialogue 1: Going to the Woods

Talker: I've been going out a lot to trails that lead through the woods, and walking along them, exploring where they go. It makes me happy to do that.

Listener: So you're saying that you're really enjoying hiking out in nature, huh.

Talker: Yes. I've been getting into trail maintenance, also. There's a nature preserve where the trails were getting really overgrown with brush. I've been spending a lot of time cutting back the undergrowth so that people can hike the trails.

Listener: What I hear you saying is that you're not only hiking the trails; you're also keeping trails cleared so other people can use them.

Talker: Right. And this gives me lots of really good exercise. Between sawing, clipping, chopping, and walking, I get a very long and hard workout.

Listener: In other words, this is a good way for you to get and stay in shape, also.

Talker: Yes. But if I were just looking for exercise, I could get it without going anywhere. I have all sorts of exercises I can do right in my room at home.

Listener: So if I understand you right, it's very possible to get exercise without going out to the woods, so there's some other attraction to it.

Talker: Right. There's something that also makes it worth it for me to check carefully and wash myself thoroughly as soon as I get back, to make sure that I didn't pick up a tick and risk Lyme Disease.

Listener: It sounds like whatever draws you to the woods is strong, because you're willing not just to spend the time, but to risk getting sick from the bugs.

Talker: Yes. Some researchers reported a study that people who were able to be in nature more were happier and not as worried. They studied lots of people.

Listener: Are you saying that some scientific writing you've seen suggests that nature helps people's mental health?

Talker: Yes. Maybe it's because our ancestors spent so much time outside in nature, that our brains evolved to feel like we belong there or something. I don't know. But for some reason, being in the woods makes me happy.

Listener: You're saying that it could be something built into almost all people's brains, or maybe not, but you're sure that for you, spending time in the woods makes you happy.

Talker: Right! Thanks for listening to me!

42. Here's another sample dialogue for the reflections exercise. As before, we depart momentarily from the format of reading a section and answering a question on it. The format I recommend is that one person (for example, the tutor) reads the part of the "talker" and the other person (for example, the student) reads the part of the "listener."

Dialogue 2: Deciding Whom to Believe

Talker: I've had a problem with some friends of mine at school. It's been a real challenge.

Listener: So you're saying that there's been a difficult situation with the relationships lately, huh?

Talker: Yes. But I think I've made some headway on it. In fact I'm feeling pretty OK about how I've handled it.

Listener: What I hear you saying is that you've made progress on this, that you feel good about.

Talker: Right. What happened was that one of my friends started telling me that another of my friends didn't like me, and that this person was saying bad things about me to other people.

Level 2

Listener: In other words, you got the word from friend number 1 that friend number 2 was putting you down.

Talker: Right. But friend number 2 was always nice to me. And we always had a good time together. And I know that friend number 1 can be a jealous person.

Listener: If I understand you right, it was at least possible that friend 1 was trying to turn you and friend 2 against each other.

Talker: That's right. So when I was with friend 2, I started listening carefully. Did they ever say bad things about other people behind their backs? I didn't hear any of that.

Listener: It sounds like you got some evidence that friend 2 was not into putting people down, generally.

Talker: Correct. And then I thought back over everything I'd heard friend 1 say, and I listened more to the things they said, and I realized that this person has said a fair number of things that I know weren't true.

Listener: Are you saying that you also got some evidence that friend 1 didn't always tell the truth?

Talker: Yes. And then one time all three of us were together, and friend 2 acted nice, but friend 1 seemed to be trying to get me not to pay any attention to friend 2. It was strange.

Listener: You're saying that when you watched the two of them when you were all together, friend 1 seemed jealous while friend 2 seemed friendly.

Talker: Yes. So I've decided not to believe any bad things about friend 2 unless I see them myself. And I've decided to try to check out what friend 1 tells me before I automatically believe it. I'm not rejecting either one of them, but I'm not letting friend 1 turn me against friend 2.

Listener: So you're saying that you're not rejecting either of them, but you're more inclined to trust friend 2 than friend 1.

Talker: That's right. Thank you for listening to me!

43. Here's the next dialogue, to provide practice in the same way.

Dialogue 3: Video Game Disagreement

Talker: My parents keep trying to get me not to play my video games. It's a problem.

Level 2

Listener: So you're saying that there's a problem with you and your parents disagreeing about how much time you should spend with video games?

Talker: Yes. One of them said to me, "There's a world out there with disease, violence, poverty, ignorance, and destruction of the environment, and you're spending all your time playing games."

Listener: What I hear you saying is that your parents think you should be doing something that improves the world instead.

Talker: That's right. But I can't just go out and reduce violence, or cure a disease, or get rid of global warming. And as you might have noticed, they haven't succeeded at any of these things either.

Listener: In other words, it's difficult or maybe impossible for you to improve the world in certain ways.

Talker: Right. And if I volunteered for some do-gooder organization, they'd probably have me bugging people for money or something like that. I don't think it would be fun at all.

Listener: So if I understand you right, you're guessing that trying to work for world peace or something like that would be unpleasant and not very useful?

Talker: That's right. And then, sitting right on my desk, is a connection to a game that is really fun to play. All I have to do is turn it on and get going, and I'm enjoying myself.

Listener: It sounds like you can count on the game to make you feel good.

Talker: I could study math, or read something good, or get a head start on the courses I'm going to take next. Yes, it would be worthwhile. But to tell you the truth, I just don't have the self-discipline to do those things when the game is right there.

Listener: Are you saying that even though doing some studying and learning would feel good, pulling yourself away from the game to do that would just take too much self-control?

Talker: Yes. I guess I'm sort of like someone addicted to cigarettes or alcohol. But at least the game isn't nearly as harmful as an addiction like those.

Listener: You're saying that even though your game is sort of like an addiction, at least it's not a very harmful one.

Talker: That's correct. If I could snap my fingers and make it so that I enjoyed trying to improve the world or learning schoolwork even more than I enjoy the game, I'd do it in a heartbeat. I really would like to have more useful stuff make me feel good.

Listener: So you're saying that it would be nice if more useful stuff brought you as much pleasure as your game.

Talker: Correct. But I don't see that happening. I don't seem to be getting tired of the game, and I'm tired of most other things before I even start.

Listener: What I hear you saying is, you don't see things changing very much.

Talker: That's right. Thanks for listening!

2.2. Listing 16 skills

44. The second requirement for Level 2 is:

List from memory all 16 of the psychological skills, preferably in order, without looking at any list of them. The tutor can give a hint by saying the first letter of each skill.

"Please! Just keep her from getting nine rattlesnakes, for several little children shall calmly play closeby!" I hope you remember from the previous level what that sentence is good for. The first letter of each word gives you the first letter of each word for the 16 skills.

Here's the list, again, with the first letters.

P Productivity
J Joyousness
K Kindness
H Honesty
F Fortitude
G Good decisions (individual and joint)
N Nonviolence
R Respectful talk (not being rude)

F Friendship-building
S Self-discipline
L Loyalty
C Conservation
S Self-care
C Compliance
P Positive Fantasy Rehearsal
C Courage

What are two ways of remembering these, that you were advised to use in the chapter on Level 1?

A. Making a mental image of each, and reading them aloud every morning.
or

B. Listening to and singing the song about them, and using the mnemonic sentence.

2.3. Two big goals

45. The third requirement: Tell, again, the two main purposes that psychological skills serve, that is the goals one accomplishes by using them. These are the two big goals of OPT and what some people think of as the two big goals of life.

Sample answer: Being happy, and helping others to be happy.

2.4. Celebrations

And here's the fourth requirement: Tell 2 more celebrations that you've done, and identify the skills.

2.5. Skills stories

And the fifth: Tell 2 more skills stories, and identify the skills.

Why are these requirements repeated? Because they are so important. If you can just do as many positive examples of the skills as you can, use fantasy rehearsal to help yourself do them, and keep checking whether your actions have good effects on yourself and others, that alone is enough to help you have a really good life.

What are the three things that are repeated in this rank that were also in the first one, in addition to remembering the 16 skills and principles?

A. Remembering the two big goals, doing celebrations, and doing skills stories.
or
B. Doing the conflict resolution role-play, practicing the ways of responding to criticism, and practicing the ways of responding to provocations.

2.6. Self-talk for feelings

46. Here's the sixth requirement:

For several feeling words, make up some plausible self-talk that could be leading to that feeling.

The tester will say several words for emotions, and want you to tell some self-talk that might be leading the person to feel that emotion. For example, if the person says scared, you might say something like, 'Uh oh, there's danger, it looks like something bad might happen!'"

The other feeling words that you do the same thing with for this requirement are words like guilty, happy, sad, angry, worried, proud, grateful, determined, liking or loving, etc.

This requirement involves

A. guessing the feeling, given some self-talk,
or
B. when given a feeling, making up some self-talk that might produce that feeling.

Feelings and Thoughts

47. Being able to come up with self-talk that goes along with a certain feeling is an important skill. Let's devote some time to this one.

Here are some examples of feelings or emotions:

angry
afraid
sad
upset
guilty
ashamed
embarrassed
worried
discouraged

happy
gleeful
proud
grateful
relaxed
determined
compassionate
liking or loving

These names of feelings (otherwise known as emotions) consist of

A. one word each
or
B. several words each?

48. Here are some examples of thoughts, that are also examples of what we call self-talk:

I did a good job on that!
Uh oh, something bad might happen.
Oops, I made a mistake.
Wow, I'm really lucky!
I really want to succeed at this!
I'm going to work really hard!
That person did something really bad!

These examples happen to be

A. one word each,
or
B. several words each?

49. There are other thoughts that are not self-talk. Some of these are "mental images." For examples, you can see, hear, touch, taste, or smell things in your imagination.

In my mind I see myself getting a good grade.
I imagine having a car wreck.
I imagine people laughing at me.
I imagine someone becoming my friend and liking me.

or
In my mind I hear a song.
I remember the sound of waves on the shore.
I remember what somebody's voice sounded like.

Someone holds in mind the memory of the sights, sounds, and smells of a fire burning in a fireplace. We would call this

A. mental images
or
B. self-talk?

50. Someone named Rasheed gets taunted by a classmate, who chants, "Rasheed is stupid! Rasheed is

stupid!" Rasheed thinks, "This person is trying to make me mad. I'm not going to give them the pleasure of succeeding! I'm going to stay calm!"
We would call the words that Rasheed thinks

A. self-talk,
or
B. being afraid?

51. You might read or hear somewhere that you can't change or control your emotions. This would mean that if you feel really depressed, or if you feel super angry over little things, or if you feel hopeless, or tortured by guilt, you just have to accept those feelings. But this isn't true -- —

It is true that most people can't simply turn feelings on and off or change them like changing channels on a TV. But you can greatly influence your own emotions, even though it may take time and work! One of the ways to do this is by choosing your self-talk and choosing your mental images.
The author thinks that

A. You can't control your own emotions.
or
B. You can greatly influence your own emotions, partly by choosing your self-talk.

52. Minata gets a bad grade on a test. Minata feels depressed and hopeless. Minata starts to notice their own self-talk, and it is like this: "I'm a worthless person. I'll never succeed. This shows I'm going to be a failure all my life."

Then Minata decides to pick different self-talk. Minata starts thinking things like this: "It's just one test. It isn't so bad. If I work harder, I can do better on the next one. I'll keep thinking of ways to do better. I think I know of someone who can help me, also!"

Do you think that the new self-talk makes Minata feel

A. more depressed,
or
B. more determined and hopeful?

53. Kameen has a problem leaving the house because of worries that the stove has been left on. Kameen feels compelled to go back to check on the stove many times before leaving the house. Kameen becomes aware that as they walk out the door of the house, they are imagining coming back to find the house in flames. Kameen purposely imagines a movie of the house just sitting there, with nothing going on, while they are gone, and looking just the same when they come back.

Is Kameen changing

A. self-talk,
or
B. mental imagery?

54. Certain types of self-talk seem to produce certain emotions. Let's practice connecting up emotions and self-talk. I'll tell you an emotion, and give you two types of self-talk. Your job is to figure out which self-talk the person is more likely to be thinking, if the person is feeling a certain way.

Here's the first one: the person is feeling very angry. Which is more likely for the person's self talk?

A. That person did something really bad! They shouldn't have done that!
or
B. Wow, what a beautiful scene this is!

55. Here's another. The person feels scared. Which self-talk is more likely?

A. I don't like it that this person is feeling bad. I want to help the person feel better.
or
B. Oh no, looks like something really bad might happen!

56. The person feels guilty and ashamed. Which self-talk is more likely?

A. I have received many blessings in life.
or
B. I have done something wrong. I shouldn't have done that.

57. A person feels surprised. Which self-talk do you think is more likely to lead to an emotion of surprise?

A. Oh! I didn't think that was going to happen!
or
B. Well, whatever. It doesn't really make much difference.

58. A person feels compassion and sympathy toward someone else. Which sort of self-talk do you think is more likely to be going on?

A. I wish I could make that person feel better; I really want to.
or
B. Just one more lap of running, and then I'll be done!

59. A person feels proud of doing something. Which self-talk seems more likely?

A. Wait, have I forgotten something?
or
B. Hooray, I did something good!

60. A person feels disgusted. Which self-talk would you guess is going on?

A. Ooh, that's gross. Let me get away from that.
or
B. What a fascinating place this is.

61. A person feels curious. Which self-talk seems more likely?

A. Wow, I really want to know the answer to this question. I want to find out!
or
B. I'm really glad I did a lot of hard work!

62. A person feels grateful. What self-talk would you connect more with that emotion?

A. I guess that what goes around, comes around.
or
B. Hey, that person did something really kind for me.

63. Which self-talk would you connect more with the emotion of embarrassment?

A. Oh no, people are looking at me and thinking I'm stupid.
or
B. Which should I pick—this one, or that other one?

64. Which self-talk do you think would lead more to the emotion of having fun?

A. OK, I'll do it if you really want me to.
or
B. Whee! Yay! How nice that I get to do this!

65. Which self-talk goes with the emotion of determination, or feeling determined to accomplish something?

A. That's pretty amazing, but I could never do something like that.
or
B. I really want to make this happen. And I'm going to work as hard as I need to, to reach my goal.

66. Which self-talk goes with feeling depressed or hopeless?

A. If you want me to do this for you, you'll have to do something for me in return.
or
B. Things are bad, and going to get worse, and there's nothing I can do to make things better.

67. Which self-talk do you think is more likely to go with the emotion of liking or loving someone?

A. How nice to be with this person! I want to make that person happy, just like they make me happy!
or
B. I wonder if that person can give me some directions on how to get where I'm going.

68. Which self-talk goes with feeling bored?

A. Just the same old stuff over and over. I'm not interested in it. I want to do something else, something exciting.
or
B. I don't want to get too down on that other person, because I'm not so perfect either.

69. Which goes with feeling upset?

A. That's OK. Don't worry about it. It's not the end of the world.
or
B. Hey, that's really bad! I don't like what happened!

70. Which goes with the emotion of relief?

A. Whew! I thought that bad thing would happen, but things came out OK!
or
B. I want to stay cool. Just breathe slowly.

71. Why are we drilling on the connection between self-talk and emotions? Because by picking your self-talk well, you can feel more of the emotions that help you to be happy and to make other people happy.

Those helpful emotions are sometimes not pleasant ones. For example, sometimes, when there is real danger present, the emotion of fear signals that danger to us and motivates us to protect ourselves. Sometimes, when we have done bad behaviors, the emotion of guilt signals to us that we have done something wrong and motivates us to do better.

So which emotions are preferable to feel at any given time is complicated. But the more your self-talk is sensible and wise, the better your emotional life will be.

What's a main point the author just made?

A. If someone feels so depressed that they can't even get out of bed and want to die, it's hard to argue that this emotion is useful.
or
B. Sensible and wise self-talk tends to lead to more useful emotions, and this is why it's good to be aware of your self-talk and how it connects with how you feel.

72. Now let's practice connecting self-talk with emotions, in the other direction. I'll tell you someone's

self-talk, and you decide which of two emotions the person is likely to be feeling.

Someone is carrying a tray of food, and someone else, horsing around, sneaks up and yells at them and touches them. The person is startled and spills stuff off the tray, and people laugh.

The person thinks, "You stupid jerk! I want to punish you, and all you losers who are laughing at this, too!"

With this self-talk, is it more likely that the person feels

A. angry,
or
B. relieved?

73. Someone has an article to write. The person thinks, "I just don't feel like doing this. I can't motivate myself. It's no use. I think I'm going to have to give up."

With this self-talk, do you think the person feels

A. determined,
or
B. discouraged?

74. Suppose that a person with an article to write thinks, "I don't feel like doing this, but that's tough! I'll do it

anyway! When I get this done, I'll celebrate a real self-discipline triumph!"

With this self-talk, do you think the person feels

A. determined,
or
B. discouraged?

75. A group of teenagers pressure Lisando really hard to drink a lot of alcohol, but Lisando refuses. Then they act really nasty to Lisando. Lisando thinks, "They put me in a tough situation, but I triumphed! I made a good decision, despite all the pressure they put on me!"

This self-talk probably led Lisando to feel

A. proud,
or
B. lonely?

76. Suppose Lisando's self-talk had been like this: "How did things get to be like this, that drinking alcohol is so important among so many people? How unfortunate that we all don't have better ways of connecting with each other."

This self-talk is more likely to go with feelings of

A. guilt,
or
B. sadness?

77. Suppose Lisando's self-talk had been like this: "I'm so lucky that my dad gave me a great model of knowing how to have fun without drinking, and of taking care of himself really well. He also taught me the facts about what alcohol does. I have a good dad."

This self-talk is more likely to go with feelings of

A. gratitude or thankfulness,
or
B. regret?

78. Serla is riding in a car, and the driver is going way too fast. If Serla were to be thinking, "Whee, yahoo, go faster, I like it," the emotion would likely be

A. having fun,
or
B. fear and worry?

79. Suppose that instead, Serla were thinking, "Oh no, we could all get killed! This is super dangerous! I need to escape this situation somehow!" Then the emotion would likely be

A. having fun,
or
B. fear and worry?

80. Suppose that instead, Serla were thinking, "Driver, what do you think you're doing! Quit your stupid thrill-seeking, you selfish brat!" Then the emotion would likely be

A. depression,
or
B. anger?

81. Trent has a deal with his parents that he gets to play a video game for a certain number of minutes in return for doing some good things that take self-discipline. At the end of the time, his parent says, "OK Trent, time's up." Suppose Trent thinks to himself, "No! You don't understand! I'm right in the middle of something! This isn't fair!" With this self-talk, Trent would be more likely to feel

A. relieved,
or
B. angry?

82. Suppose that instead, Trent said to himself, "OK, let me remind myself that this deal we have is really helping me to use self-discipline and do good things.

My parent is doing me a favor by working with me on this."

With this self-talk, Trent would be more likely to feel

A. scared,
or
B. grateful?

83. Suppose that instead, Trent said to himself, "This is hard, because I'm right in the middle of something. But I can get tough! I'm going to do it, and get off! This is going to be a self-discipline triumph!"

With this self-talk, Trent would be more likely to feel

A. determined,
or
B. sad?

84. Mental images can affect how we feel, just as self-talk can. Let's drill just a little bit on that connection.

Ling is about to give a speech. Suppose that while waiting, Ling has a picture in mind of forgetting what comes next, and everyone in the audience looking at each other and laughing at him. With this image in mind, Ling is more likely to feel

A. loving,

or
B. nervous?

85. Suppose that instead, Ling runs through the mind a movie of giving the speech enthusiastically and well, just as in the practice sessions that Ling has done. With this imagery in mind, Ling is more likely to feel

A. confident,
or
B. compassionate?

86. Suppose that in class, Noro gets the urge to talk out and say something pretty disrespectful of a certain politician, that may also be funny. But Noro hasn't done this yet. Suppose Noro flashes on the image of the teacher's getting really mad, and the classmates rolling their eyes and one of them saying "How immature." With this imagery, Noro is more likely to feel

A. relieved at having resisted the urge,
or
B. enthusiastic about going ahead and talking out?

87. Suppose that instead, Noro had flashed on the image of everyone laughing, including the teacher, and someone sitting in the next seat doing a high five. With this imagery, Noro is more likely to feel

A. relieved at having resisted the urge,
or
B. enthusiastic about going ahead and talking out?

88. Sindham works a little at a computer in a library. Sindham imagines germs getting on their fingers and then getting onto everything else they touch. With this imagery, Sindham is likely to feel

A. worried,
or
B. proud?

89. Suppose that instead, Sindham imagines telling someone about the interesting stuff that they learned while on the computer at the library, and imagines the person feeling really glad to hear about it. With this imagery, Sindham is more likely to feel

A. friendly,
or
B. scared?

90. Many people go through their whole lives without really becoming aware of how their self-talk and their mental imagery influence their emotions. Many people go through life without really consciously noticing what their self-talk and their mental imagery are, in the first place! If you can notice what your self-talk and mental

imagery are, and how they affect your emotions, you will be way ahead of the game! Learning this sort of thing has helped many, many people to be happier and to make others happier!

The author thinks that noticing your own self-talk and mental imagery and how they connect with how you feel

A. will just make you too wrapped up in yourself,
or
B. is a helpful thing to start doing, early in life?

2.7. Brainstorming options

91. Here's the last requirement for level 2:

Given a choice point situation, take turns with someone listing options. Together, come up with at least 6 reasonable options.

A number of research studies have found that being able to think up lots of reasonable options is an important skill for mental health. This finding makes sense, doesn't it? A good life depends on making good decisions. It's hard to decide to do a good option if you haven't even thought about that option in the first place.

Thinking up options is very much like the divergent thinking exercise. The question is: Someone was in this situation. They thought of a reasonable thing to do. What did they think of?

How do you teach yourself to think of lots of good options? I recommend practicing by using these steps:

1. Reading about a problem or choice point.
2. Thinking up as many options as you can.
3. Reading the list of options that someone else generated for that situation.
4. For the options that you left out, thinking, "What type of option was this?"

A point the author makes in this section is that

A. The ability to think up lots of good options is a skill that helps people to be mentally healthy.
or
B. Once one has a good list of options, a next step in decision making is to think about the advantages and disadvantages of those options.

92. When thinking of options, there's one type that doesn't count: violent options. I can't say that trying to hurt someone is absolutely never a smart or good thing to do. But in my seven decades of living so far, I have never yet run into one situation where my being violent was a good idea. As the world progresses, hopefully the times where violence is useful will be even less frequent. In addition, the exposure to violent options

through games and movies and TV shows and violent sports is so great that no one needs to be reminded that violence is an option.

The author's attitude toward violence is

A. It's good to be skilled at it, so as to protect yourself.
or
B. If you make good choices and are lucky, you may be able to completely avoid either giving or receiving it.

Level 3

3.1. Four ways of listening

93. The first challenge for level 3 is as follows:

List four ways of listening to another person, that are used in conversation, in addition to telling about your own experience.

The four ways of listening are:

1. reflections
2. facilitations
3. follow-up questions
4. positive feedback

If two people use these, and if they take turns telling about their own experience as well, they usually have a good conversation! I remember **Reflections**, telling about your own **Experience**, **Facilitations**, **Follow-up questions**, and positive **Feedback** by the letters REFFF.

In REFFF, what do the three F's stand for?

A. facilitations, feedback, and follow-up.

or
B. fancy, fun, and fulfilling?

94. Let's review very quickly what these four responses are. When you read these, I recommend letting the student read the listener's part, and the tutor read the rest.

Here's an example of a Reflection:
Talker: I get so discouraged watching the news these days.
Listener: Seeing the bad things happening in the world gets you down, huh.

Here's an example of a facilitation:
Talker: I see people doing bad things, and other people who don't seem to care, and who support them anyway.
Listener: Um humh. I see.

Here's an example of a follow-up question:
Talker: I just wonder if the values that I thought most people could agree on are not something we really agree on.
Listener: Which values are you thinking about?

Here's an example of positive feedback:
Talker: I'm thinking for example of telling the truth. People who are our leaders say things pretty often that

just aren't true. I've checked lots of the things very carefully and found that they are lies.
Listener: I'm glad you take the time to check carefully. Lots of people don't have the energy to do that.

If the listener says: oh, unh hunh, yes, right, humh, OK, or I see, that listener is doing a

A. facilitation,
or
B. reflection?

3.2. Listening with 4 responses

95. Here's the second challenge for level 3:

When someone reads you the thoughts and utterances of an imaginary person, and gives you one of the four ways of listening, be able to give a good example of using that response to respond to what the person said.

Here's a conversation to practice that with. Tutor, please read the talker's part, and student, please read the listener's part.

Talker: I learned something really important while I was learning to read, that wasn't just about reading. (Please use a follow-up question.)
Listener: What important thing did you learn?

Talker: My reading tutor said it many times to me: "Repetition is the learner's friend." (Please use a facilitation.)
Listener: Oh, I see.

Talker: By this my tutor meant that practicing things over and over is the way to get good at doing things. At the beginning, if tutor asked me to read a list of words over again, I would say, "But I've already done that!" As if that somehow meant I didn't need to do it again. (Please use a reflection.)
Listener: So at the beginning, you thought that if you practiced a word list once, you should be able to remember it for the rest of your life and not practice it again, huh?

Talker: My tutor told me about all sorts of people who needed to practice things hundreds or thousands of times. Basketball players who practiced shooting. Singers or musicians who rehearsed every day. Runners who ran just about every day. Students who practiced answering sample test questions over and over. (Please use a reflection.)
Listener: So your tutor gave you many examples of people who succeeded because they were willing to practice over and over many times.

Talker: Yes. And eventually I came to believe it. And I used that idea, not just in reading. I used it to get really fast and accurate at math facts. I used it when I learned how to type on a computer keyboard, using the correct fingers on the keys. It was really helpful to me. (Please use a positive feedback.)
Listener: It's great that you developed the self-discipline to practice things over and over! Congratulations!

Talker: Thank you!

There's no A or B question for this text unit.

96. Now here's a chance for the student to practice listening with four responses. Tutor, please read the talker's part, and student, please make up your own example of a reflection, facilitation, follow-up question, or positive feedback after each thing that the talker says. You get to pick which of the four feels best to do. Try to at least one of each of the four. Tutor, if the student asks a follow-up question, just make up an answer to it and then go on to the next thing the talker says.

Talker: I have come to be able to sleep lots better than I did before. I'm really pleased with how well the plan I used has worked.

(Listener, please say one of the four listening responses, after this and after each of the other things the talker says.)

Talker: I used to go to sleep listening to music. I learned that it's a better idea to go to sleep with the same thing going on that you will find in the middle of the night if you wake up. That way you can fall back asleep in the conditions under which you're used to falling asleep.

Talker: I also used to get up really late some mornings after going to bed really late. That used to make it hard for me to fall asleep at an earlier time again. Now I keep the time I go to bed and get up really steady.

There's no question for this text unit!

97. The conversation continues:

Talker: Before I learned more about sleep, I read and watched videos in bed a lot. Now I know that I want to make it that the bed is a signal for me to get to sleep, and so if I do anything other than sleep, I do it out of the bed.

Talker: If I wake up in the middle of the night and can't get back to sleep, I get up and do something useful but not very exciting. I study a school book, for example. Then when I'm sleepy I go back to bed.

Talker: I used to get exercise some days and not on other days. Now I make a point of getting a good bit of exercise every single day, so that by the time I go to bed I'm tired.

Talker: One more thing I've done is to practice relaxing in the daytime, so I can use that skill at night. I also practice making up pleasant dream-like fantasies of kindness, happiness, beauty, and relaxation, so that I can enjoy doing these while I'm lying in bed relaxing.

Talker: I used to try really hard to go to sleep. Now I realize that it's best to just enjoy the time relaxing in bed, and not to worry about whether I fall asleep or not.

No question for this text unit either. Listener, I hope you got good practice coming up with the 4 listening responses!

3.3. Sixteen skills and principles

98. Here's the next challenge for Level 3:

Say from memory all sixteen skills and principles, including the two separate parts of the sixth one (good decisions). Do it without looking at any list. Say again what two big goals psychological skills help people achieve.

Level 3

Have you learned to sing the song yet that helps you remember the 16 skills? And have you found that the sentence "Please just keep her from getting nine rattlesnakes, for several little children shall calmly play closeby" helps in remembering? PJKHFGNR FSLCSCPC stand for: productivity, joyousness, kindness, honesty, fortitude, good decisions, nonviolence, respectful talk, friendship building, self-discipline, loyalty, conservation, self-care, compliance, positive fantasy rehearsal, and courage.

What are the two parts of good decisions? One is good "individual decisions," where you are deciding what YOU should do. The second skill is good "joint decisions," where you and someone else, or you and more than one other person, are making a decision together, looking for an option you can agree on doing. Joint decisions includes "conflict resolution" -- where people at first disagree on what to do, and it's good if they can find something they agree on.

Suppose one person needs to study, and the other needs to practice their violin. The violin playing is distracting the person studying. They talk together about what they should do. Is this

A. an individual decision,
or
B. a joint decision?

99. What are the 16 skills meant to help you do? What are the two big goals, for OPT and, according to some people, for life?

To be happy and help others to be happy. To care for yourself and care for others. To be good to yourself, and to be good to other people.

What's one more way of saying the same thing?

A. To have a sound mind in a sound body.
or
B. To act with loving kindness toward yourself and toward your fellow human beings.

3.4. Celebrations

100. Here's the fourth challenge for Level 3:

Tell 3 more celebrations and identify the skills.

You've already done this for each of the two preceding ranks. Why do it again? Because there is no limit to the number of different positive examples of psychological skills that you can come up with to do. Trying to do as many as you can is a good "game" to play for the rest of your life!

Here's an example of a celebration:

Just a while ago, while I was writing, I reminded myself to stretch up tall rather than slumping over in my chair, at least for a while. I practiced having good posture. Self-care, and some self-discipline.

Remember that celebrations are smart or good things that you have actually done. Skills stories are smart or good things that you've read about, heard about, or make up.

One time in real life someone said, "You're just a baby! You haven't grown up at all yet!" I handled it without losing my cool. I think that was an example of fortitude. Is this a

A. celebration,
or
B. skills story?

3.5. Skills stories

101. Here's the fifth challenge for level 3:

When the tester names a random psychological skill, tell a skills story modeling that skill, for 3 different stories about 3 different skills.

It's great to make up skills stories. But they can also be stories you remember from any other source. Skills stories don't have to be long or elaborate. Here's what they can sound like:

Tutor: Productivity.
Student: There was a beaver, and it wanted to build a house for itself and its family. So it spent a lot of time chewing branches off fallen trees and putting them in just the right place, and finally it finished its house.

Tutor: That's a good one. How about self-discipline?
Student: Someone in a family had cooked some food that this person wanted to eat the next day. The person's brother saw it in the refrigerator and thought it would taste really good. But the brother didn't eat it, to be nice to his family member.

Tutor: Good. How about nonviolence?
Student: Some people on social media were mad at the police and trying to get lots of people to throw things at police. But a kid named Rayta wrote on social media and explained why this was not a good strategy and talked about better things people could do instead.

Is it against the rules to tell a skills story you've read in Illustrated Stories That Model Psychological Skills or Programmed Readings for Psychological Skills? (Answer is in the 3rd sentence in this section!)

A. Yes,
or
B. No?

3.6. Remembering the 12 thoughts

102. Here's the 6th challenge for level 3:

Be able to recite what the twelve thoughts are, from memory.

Be sure you understand the difference between the 16 skills and the 12 thoughts! The 12 thoughts are types of sentences you say to yourself. If you pick wisely among them, they will help you in carrying out behaviors that are examples of the 16 skills.

I remember the 12 thoughts in sets of 3. The first 3 are thinking about how something is bad or undesirable. Awfulizing is thinking that the situation you're in is bad or undesirable. Getting down on yourself is thinking that you or your own actions are bad or undesirable. Blaming someone else is thinking that someone else or their actions are bad or undesirable. The second three are just decisions not to do, or overdo, the first 3. Stick a "not" before the first three and you have the second three: not awfulizing, not getting down on yourself, and not blaming someone else. The next three are the "logical thinking" group. You form a goal (goal-setting), you decide how to try to reach it (listing options and choosing), and you notice what happened and learn for next time (learning from the experience). The last three are thinking about how something is good or desirable: the situation, just by chance (celebrating luck), someone else's action (celebrating someone else's choice) or your own action (celebrating your own choice).

The author thinks of the 12 thoughts as

A. four sets, with three thoughts in each set,
or
B. 3 sets, with four thoughts in each set?

3.7. Identify types of thoughts

103. Here's the seventh challenge for level 3.

When you are given examples of thoughts, be able to correctly tell which of the 12 thoughts each is an example of, without being given two options to choose from.

Have you read the Journey Story in Programmed Readings, and the chapter after that on the 12 thought exercise? If so, you should be really familiar with figuring out which of the 12 thoughts a certain thought represents.

Here are some examples.

Someone has a basketball coach. The coach makes the person do a certain drill over and over. The person thinks, "That coach is just mean! That coach likes to make people do things that aren't fun, just because they like power!"

What type of thought is that?

104. In the previous section, the answer was blaming someone else. Here's another example. Someone's refrigerator stops working. The person thinks, "Oh, darn it! I just can't take one more thing gone wrong!"

What type of thought is that?

105. For the previous section, the answer was awfulizing. Here's a third example: Someone has an appointment to keep by phone. The person sets an alarm on their phone to remind them of the appointment time. This works, and the person keeps the appointment successfully. The person thinks, "Hooray, my plan really worked well! I am going to make use of that in the future!"

What type of thought was that? There are two possible correct answers.

106. For the previous section, the two correct answers were celebrating your own choice and learning from the experience.

3.8. Purpose of twelve thought classification

Here's the 8th challenge for level 3.

Explain what the purpose of the 12 thought classification is.

The purpose of learning about the 12 thoughts is to help us choose better what is most helpful for us to think—to choose better what we want to say to ourselves! Sometimes one is more useful, and sometimes another. Even awfulizing, getting down on ourselves, and blaming other people can sometimes be useful ways to think, especially if we don't overdo it too much. If we have names for these types of thoughts, it's much easier for us to make choices between them.

Why is it important to make good choices about how to think? Because how we think has a lot to do with how we feel. It also has a lot to do with how we behave. Thinking about the world in useful ways helps us have feelings that are good for us, and to pick behaviors that are good to do.

One of the points made in the unit you just read is that

A. The 12 thought classification helps us make good choices on what to say to ourselves.
or
B. It would be possible to make up other types of thoughts, such as "describing what is observed,"

"predicting consequences," and "posing questions to yourself." But you have to stop somewhere, and these 12 are enough to really help.

3.9. Which reflection is better

107. Here's the ninth requirement for level 3.

When given pairs of reflections that someone could make to the same utterance, consistently tell which reflection is better.

You've done the reflections exercise for previous ranks. This time please focus on recognizing "high quality" or "good" reflections. What makes a good reflection?

1. You reflect back the part of what the other person says that is most important, not the less important details.
2. Your reflection is accurate—you don't say back things that the person didn't say or mean.
3. You don't reflect in a way that disapproves or editorializes about what the person says.
4. Your reflection is concise—you don't say back every little thing the other person says in a fairly long utterance, even if you have a good enough memory to do so.

5. Your reflection makes the other person feel understood and that you have empathy—to do this you usually need to be gentle and polite.

This unit says that reflections should be:

A. slow, low, and without much inflection of pitch.
or
B. Nice, accurate, and short enough.

108. Please pick the better reflection of the two.

Talker: I get so sleepy sometimes in the middle of the day. But then, when it's time to go to bed, I feel wide awake. It's frustrating.

A. Listener: If I understand you correctly you get sleepy in the middle of the day.
or
B. Listener: It sounds like you'd like to be less sleepy in the day and more sleepy when you go to bed.

109. In the previous section, the second choice summarized the whole point the speaker made rather than just a part of it, and was the better reflection.

Now please pick the better reflection for the following utterance.

Level 3

Talker: I read about how people who are really great at what they do spend huge amounts of time practicing. Basketball or other sports stars, musicians, doctors, mathematicians, and others. But I can't seem to get motivated to spend a lot of time practicing anything. I just get bored too quickly and can't keep up the work.

A. Listener: You'd like for your work capacity to be higher, so that you can get more skill and accomplish more?
or
B. Listener: You're saying that you're too lazy to practice enough to be great at something, right?

110. In the previous text unit, the second reflection was phrased in a way that probably sounded insulting to the speaker; the other one was better.

Please pick the better reflection for the following.

Talker: When I hear of these basketball stars spending lots of hours practicing each day, on the one hand I admire them. But on the other hand, I think, what does the world really need now? Does it need people who can throw a ball through a hoop really well? What if people spent as much practice time learning to do things that really make people lots better off?

A. Listener: You admire people who can work very hard, for example at sports skills, but you would admire even more people who work at the skills that make life better, more than sports do.
or
B. Listener: You think basketball players are wasting their time doing stuff that is unnecessary and they should work on something else instead, because when you come down to it, their work doesn't do anybody any good, and people waste too much time on sports, and who cares who wins or loses a bunch of stupid games?

111. In the previous text unit, in the second reflection the listener went on for a little too long and made a statement that was more extreme than the speaker's statement was. Therefore the other was better.

Please pick the better reflection for the following utterance.

Talker: To me, both spinach and mushrooms are OK, but nothing particularly great. But there's an Indian restaurant that puts together a dish with spinach and mushrooms and spices and other stuff, and it's just great! I love it! It's amazing to me that that they can do that.

A. Listener: So you're saying that sometimes you don't like spinach and mushrooms, but other times you do.
or

B. Listener: So it's amazing to you that these Indian chefs can take vegetables that are by themselves not that appetizing, and put them together in a way that tastes really good to you!

112. In the previous text unit, the second reflection recognizes the feelings of amazement and delight about the accomplishment of the chefs, whereas the first one misses all that.

Please pick the better reflection for the following utterance.

Talker: Reading history, I find it really sad and disappointing how many wars have been fought and how many people have been killed because people didn't like other people's religions. And this is even though most of those religions have tried to teach the values of love and kindness and peace.

A. Listener: It's disappointing to you how many times people have used religion as an excuse for violence, even when the religions teach nonviolence.
or
B. Listener: In other words you're saying that religion causes people to kill each other.

113. In the previous text unit, the second reflection oversimplifies what the speaker says, and refers only to

half of a balanced pair of points the speaker is making. The other is better.

3.10. Brainstorming options

Here's the last requirement for level 3.

Given a choice point, take turns thinking of options. Together, come up with at least 8 reasonable options.

Being able to think of lots of reasonable options in the choice points that come up in your life is an extremely useful skill. Making good choices is very important, and it's hard to choose a good option if you don't think of it in the first place!

Here are some general types of options you might consider.

1. It's always an option just not to do anything.
2. You can go to an expert to get help.
3. You can go to an organization to get help.
4. You can look up information on the Internet that might help.
5. You can use a technological or scientific solution.
6. You can get work at a skill that will help solve the problem.
7. You can teach someone else a skill that will help solve the problem.

8. You can figure out how to use reward or non-reward to change behavior for the better.
9. You can figure out how to use penalties to change behavior.
10. You can appeal to the rule of law or authority.
11. You can somehow get into a different situation to escape the problem.

The types of options mentioned in this unit

A. Are meant to solve a certain particular problem,
or
B. Are general types of solutions that you can at least consider for lots of different types of problems?

114. Let's apply the types of solutions mentioned above to a particular problem. Let's say that the problem is that a family member drinks too much alcohol, and the family member does mean and harmful things when they are drunk. Let's look at the list above, and list a specific option for each of the types listed above.

1. You could just ignore the problem and do nothing.
2. You could consult a doctor who specializes in alcoholism, or try to get your family member to consult that expert.
3. You could try to get your family member to go to a group like Alcoholics Anonymous, or go to a group like Al-Anon yourself.

4. You could search on the Internet for more information on things people have done.
5. You could see if the person is willing to take any of several drugs that have been found useful in treating alcoholism.
6. You can work at the skill of staying calm and reasonable yourself, even when someone else is acting unreasonably.
7. You can teach the family member skills of self-discipline or relaxation or mood regulation or any other skills that would help them, if you can learn how to teach those skills.
8. If the family member gets money from you, you can make the money come only when the person has not drunk anything for a certain length of time.
9. You can punish the person for buying alcohol (and at the same time make it unavailable) by just pouring it down the sink every time you find it in the house, after searching for it daily.
10. If the person drinks and drives, you can let the police know that the person is driving so that the person will get some penalties for drinking.
11. If you live with this family member, you can move away.

What did we do in this section?

Level 3

A. We took the general ways of solving problems listed in the previous section, and applied them to a certain specific problem.
or
B. We just listed a bunch of ways to solve a problem, in a way that didn't have anything to do with the previous section.

115. Now let's take the same general ways of solving a problem, and apply them to another different choice point. The problem is that I have transferred from a school that went slowly in math, to a school that goes much faster, and I find that I am behind.

1. I could just try to do my work without doing anything specific about this problem.
2. I could find someone who is good at math to help me out.
3. I could sign up with an organization that tutors people in math.
4. I could look on the Internet for ways of catching up in math.
5. I see that scientists have found that testing yourself is a good way to help your memory, so I could use that finding in trying to learn math.
6. I could buy and use a book or more than one book to teach myself math skills.

7. If the person helping me gets impatient too quickly, I could help them learn to be more patient with me by very gently suggesting to them that they do so.
8. I could reward myself for doing extra work on math by letting myself eat my favorite food only after I've done so.
9. When I haven't worked on math, I could penalize myself by not letting myself do fun stuff on screens.
10. I could go to the teacher or principal or ask my parents to do so, and let them know about the problem, and ask them to come up with a solution that will help me.
11. I could try to get into a different math class that isn't so over my head, or substitute tutoring for going to math class altogether.

What did we do in this section?

A. We took the same general ways of solving a problem that we listed two sections ago, and applied them to a different specific problem.
or
B. We just listed a bunch of options for solving a problem, that didn't have anything to do with any prior list.

Level 4

4.1. Twelve thought exercise

116. Here's the first requirement for Level 4.

Do the 12 thought exercise, for a situation the tester gives you, coming up with each of the 12 thoughts yourself, without the tester prompting you by telling you the names of the thoughts. In other words, do a 12 thought exercise totally on your own.

If you've read about the 12 thoughts and the exercise in the various manuals, you've gotten lots of tips on how and why to do the 12 thought exercise. Here are some quick reminders:

1. For awfulizing, getting down on yourself, and blaming someone else, you can "overdo it" or "overgeneralize" if you want, or you can avoid overdoing it. Both are useful to you; just try to be aware of which you're doing.
2. For "not awfulizing," you don't have to deny that the situation is bad. You can just remind yourself that it is not bad enough to keep you from handling it the best you can.
3. For "not getting down on yourself" and "not blaming someone else," you don't have to deny any fault

in yourself or someone else. You can just remind yourself that you can use your energy in other ways.

4. For goal-setting, think about what you can reasonably wish would happen either in this situation or after this situation is over.

5. For listing options and choosing, try to think about three or four reasonable options, not just a bad one and a good one. You can think about pros and cons too if you want. Don't forget to say what option you pick.

Someone is doing the 12 thought exercise. The person says, "One option is that I could hit the other person; another option is that I could just ignore what they said. I think I'll just ignore it." This is listing options and choosing, but is it doing it in the best way, mentioned above?

A. yes,
or
B. no?

117. Here are some more tips on the 12 thought exercise.

6. When you are learning from the experience, it's OK to be reminded of something you already knew. It's also OK to just have a possibility raised in your mind, without coming to a firm conclusion. For example, someone eats and drinks a lot of dairy products, and

their skin breaks out. The person says, "I learned from this to *consider* the *possibility* that the dairy products are not good for my skin."

7. When celebrating luck, when something bad happens, it's always possible to celebrate that it was not even worse.

8. How do you celebrate someone else's choice when someone has done something bad to you? You can celebrate the choices of the people who didn't do that bad thing to you, or the choices of the people who have been nice to you! And it's also possible to make up a good action of another character in the story!

9. How do you celebrate your own choice when the situation is that you've made a mistake or done something bad? You can celebrate the good way you've chosen to try to make things better in the present or the future. Or you can celebrate having forgiven yourself for your mistake.

Suppose the situation is that someone ran into your parked car with their big truck, totally destroyed the car, and drove off in their truck. You want to celebrate someone else's choice. What's an example of following the suggestion above?

A. I'm glad the person did that; I was ready to get a new car anyway.
or

B. I appreciate the people who have driven carefully and not done things like that. And I really celebrate the person who got that person's license plate number and wrote it down for me.

118. When you're doing the 12 thought exercise, it's sometimes a good idea to "add on" to the situation by imagining something else that happened in addition. But don't change or undo the original situation to make it easier to come up with one of the thoughts.

The situation is that your house burned down. Which is the better way to "celebrate luck?"

A. I'm lucky that my insurance policy covers things like this, and will make a big payment.
or
B. Isn't this lucky: I was just dreaming, and my house didn't burn down at all.

4.2. Dr. L.W. Aap

119. Here's the second requirement for level 4.

Tell from memory what Dr. L.W. Aap stands for, and tell why each element of Dr. L.W. Aap tends to help people make better joint decisions or resolve conflict better.

Here's what the letters stand for: Defining, Reflecting, Listing, Waiting, Advantages, Agreeing, and Politeness.

Here's how each element helps:

Defining the problem or defining your point of view without blaming or bossing the other person brings up the topic while minimizing how mad or defensive you make the other person. It tries to set the stage for a "rational" conversation in which people are looking for a solution to the problem rather than a way of attacking or defeating the other person.

Reflecting lets the other person hear that you have understood their point of view about the problem. If you understood it wrong, it lets you both try again to make things clear.

Listing options is really useful because it's hard to agree on the best solution to the problem if no one has thought it up in the first place!

Waiting until you're finished listing before you start criticizing the options gives you more time to think about good things to possibly do, without getting bogged down arguing about some option that may pretty obviously not be the best one anyway.

Advantages and disadvantages keeps you thinking about the options, and helps you figure out which one is best, and stays away from the question of which person is the better person!

Agreeing on something is a very desirable outcome of a joint decision or conflict-resolution conversation.

Politeness helps people stay rational and not get into a lot of fighting language. Plus, almost everyone enjoys it when people have been polite to them.

Which of the 7 elements of Dr. L.W. Aap is the one where you think about the pros and cons of the various plans?

A. advantages and disadvantages
or
B. reflecting?

4.3. Joint decision role-play

120. Here's the third requirement for Level 4.

Role-play a Dr. L.W. Aap conversation with the tester, given a joint decision situation of the tester's choosing, in which each of you do all 7 elements of Dr. L.W. Aap.

There are examples of how to do this in Programmed Readings, the Exercises book, and the Conflict-Resolution and Anger Control Book. But here's one more example of what a Dr. L.W. Aap conversation might sound like. I'll try to be brief. There's no question on this section. I recommend that the tutor take one part, and the student take the other part, and you read this with each other as in a play.

Person 1: May I talk with you about a problem, my next door neighbor? Your family likes to build fires outside and sit around them. But the fires are close to our house, and the smoke comes in our house and yard. (Defining)

Person 2: If I understand you correctly, the smoke from our fires bothers you. (Reflecting)

Person 1: That's right.

Person 2: For some reason people just seem to find it fun to be around a wood fire at night, telling stories and singing songs and so forth. For that reason we would hate to give it up. (Defining)

Person 1: You're saying that for you and your friends, the fire seems to bring out good times. (Reflecting)

Person 2: Right.

Person 1: One option is that you could get some extension cords and some fans, and blow the smoke in other directions. (Listing)

Person 2: Or we could build the fires only when the wind is blowing in a different direction from your house. (Listing)

Person 1: We could maybe buy an air purifier that would filter out the smoke in our house, and maybe you could chip in part of the price of it. (Listing)

Person 2: We could move our place for fires to the other side of the house. Think those are enough options? (Listing. They have Waited.)

Person 1: Yes. I like the option of moving the fireplace farther away from us. The wind is pretty changeable. And the air purifier takes a while to work. (Advantages)

Person 2: I like the same option. Trying to blow the smoke with fans probably wouldn't work if there were a breeze going your direction. (Advantages)

Person 1: How about we give a try to moving the place of your fires, and see how that works out?

Person 2: Sounds good. Next time we have one, I'll try to remember to ask you whether it was better for you. (Agreeing)

Person 1: Thank you. (Politeness, which has also taken place throughout the conversation.)

Person 2: Thanks to you also.

4.4. Ways of reducing fear or aversion

121. Here's the fourth requirement for level 4.

Explain and give an example of how someone would use each of the following in reducing a fear or aversion: estimating the danger, staying in the scary situation long enough (prolonged exposure), choosing self-talk, relaxation, fantasy rehearsal, taking it gradually (hierarchy), working on skills.

In this one, you will be given a specific fear or aversion. The tester will prompt you for each of the above methods of reducing that fear or aversion, and you explain how the person would use that method for that specific fear or aversion.

Suppose that the specific fear or aversion was this: A person has an aversion to doing writing assignments. When the person is assigned to write something, and the person tries to write, the person gets such bad feelings that it is hard for them to go on.

Estimating the danger: The person could think: "I don't put myself in any danger at all by doing this assignment —I'm in danger of lowering my grade if I don't do it.

Maybe I'm worried about the danger of doing a bad job and being embarrassed. But that's the danger that comes from turning in a final draft that's bad. If my first draft is bad, I can always revise it. So there's really hardly any danger at all in writing my first draft."

Staying in the scary situation long enough (prolonged exposure): The person decides to work on the first draft for 25 minutes and then stop and celebrate the prolonged exposure, even if the quality of the draft is not very high.

Choosing self-talk: The person could avoid getting down on themselves by saying, "This isn't good writing," but could celebrate their own choice by saying, "Hooray, I'm glad I'm working on this!"

Relaxation: The person could, every 5 or 10 minutes or so, take 3 or 4 seconds to relax their muscles.

Fantasy rehearsal: The person could imagine themselves gradually making progress, improving the writing over time, and eventually coming up with something that is still not perfect, but good enough, and feeling really good about that.

Taking it gradually (hierarchy): The person at first could "set the bar" at just, "I want to do this well enough to pass." Then the person could shoot for getting a better and better grade. Then the person could shoot for actually getting their writing accepted for publication.

Working on skills: The person could spend time practicing touch-typing, spelling, editing grammar, combining sentences, reading about how to make outlines, learning vocabulary, practicing writing letters to people, and practicing writing essays that are graded by artificial intelligence online. All these skills would help the person feel more confident in their writing ability.

If the person noticed that they were saying very self-critical things every time they started to write, and this seemed to interfere super-greatly with their writing, which of the above do you think would be more important to do soon?

A. change the self-talk,
or
B. work on vocabulary skills?

122. Let's give another example of how you would tell how to use each of the above methods, this time with a different fear or aversion.

Suppose the person has a very strong aversion to criticism. Being criticized makes the person feel very bad—this usually comes out as the person feeling very angry for a long time.

Estimating the danger: The person could think, "If it's really true that I have a certain fault, it's better for me to know it than not to know it, so the criticism itself doesn't endanger me. If I don't have the fault that the person is criticizing me for, then it doesn't endanger me much for them to tell me their mistaken impression—maybe some social danger if they persuade other people. Either way, I'm not put in much danger to hear this."

Staying in the situation long enough: The person could ask the other person to enlarge on the criticism, by saying things like, "Oh? Tell me more, please. Tell me what suggestions you have." That way, the time of hearing the criticism stretches out long enough for them to get used to it. Or, they could do some pretty prolonged fantasy rehearsals of handling the criticism.

Choosing self-talk: The person could do less blaming the other person, and more learning from the experience, and more celebrating their choice to stay cool and calm.

Relaxation: The person could relax their jaw muscles, particularly if they find their jaw muscles clenching up when they get mad.

Level 4

Fantasy rehearsal: The person could go through a whole bunch of possible criticism and practice responding to them with the T PAARISEC options (thank you, planning to ponder or problem solve, agreeing with part of criticism, asking for more specific criticism, reflection, I want or I feel statement, silent eye contact, explaining the reason, criticizing the critic.)

Taking it gradually: The person could start practicing with very gentle criticism, and work their way up to more harsh and insulting ones.

Working on skills: The person could practice the skill of responding to criticism by having someone else make up criticisms, while the person practices responding in a cool and calm way.

In the past two sections, some people might describe the first person as being lazy and the second as having a bad temper. What point is the author making about these examples?

A. Laziness is a hard problem to solve, because you have to work to solve it.
or
B. You can work on an aversion to writing or to criticism in just the same ways that people work on fears of heights or fears of dogs etc.

4.5. Four thoughts

123. Here's the fifth requirement.

Tell the four thoughts that are used for the four-thought exercise, and do the four thought exercise for one possibly scary situation and for one situation that possibly might provoke anger.

The four thoughts are: 1. Not awfulizing 2. Goal-setting 3. Listing options and choosing, and 4. Celebrating your own choice. The author remembers this with the mnemonic, "Not gonna lose cash." The first letters of each of those four words are also the first letters of each of the four thoughts.

Here's how you would use these for a scary situation. Someone supplies you with a scary situation, as follows:

The person is going to get their teeth cleaned at the dentist's office, and the person feels scared of this situation.

Not awfulizing: I know this isn't really painful. Lots of people get this done every day and do just fine with it.

Goal-setting: My short term goal is to get through this teeth cleaning while at least appearing to be fine with the procedure (taking advantage of the fact that acting a certain way helps you feel a certain way). My long term goal is to get used to this, so that it doesn't bother me.

Listing options and choosing: I can practice relaxing my muscles, both before my appointment and during it. I can remind myself that I'm not in danger. I can fantasy rehearse speaking with the hygienist in a pleasant and friendly way. I can do that during the procedure, during the times I get to talk at any rate. I can fantasy rehearse thinking about some interesting things during the procedure, and practice that when it actually happens. I can practice biofeedback before the procedure, getting my heart rate to go down by relaxing. I can watch videos of the procedure to help myself fantasy rehearse. I can ask a family member to touch my teeth with a toothbrush, to practice handling someone else touching the inside of my mouth. Actually I think all of these are good options; I'm going to do all of them!

Celebrating your own choice: I think I came up with some good ideas about dealing with this problem!

When this person listed options, which two of them do you think were used more?

A. relaxation and fantasy rehearsal.
Or
B. slow breathing and tones of voice?

124. Now let's give an example of how you would use the four thought exercise to practice with a provocation, a situation that might make someone angry.

Here's the situation: You and your sibling have both played in a recital. Your aunt and uncle came to hear the recital. After the concert your aunt and uncle greatly praise your sibling, but they don't say anything to you, even though you played as well as your sibling.

Here we go with the four thought exercise:

Not awfulizing: This isn't awful – if my sibling gets praise, it doesn't take anything away from me. This isn't a contest between me and my sibling. If they help my sibling feel good about themselves, that's just fine.

Goal-setting: My goal is to be a magnanimous person, the type who isn't greedy for either money or praise or recognition, but who is generous and able to take pleasure in someone else's having something good happen. Also I want to be nice to all my family members, including my sibling and my aunt and uncle.

Listing options and choosing: I can join in and congratulate my sibling myself. I can say to my aunt and uncle, "Thanks for coming to this!" I can hang out with other people I enjoy, and chat with them. I can celebrate my performance in my own mind and use self-reinforcement. I think all these options are good, and I'm going to do all of them!

Celebrating my own choice: Hooray, I came up with some good plans!

What's another example of being "magnanimous"?

A. Someone gives a speech even when they are very scared to.
Or
B. Someone feels proud of a co-worker when the co-worker wins a prize for an accomplishment, rather than feeling jealous of that co-worker.

4.6. Options for joint decision

125. Here's the sixth requirement for this level.

Given a joint decision choice point situation that the tester chooses, come up with at least 6 reasonable options all by yourself.

First, let's review what a "joint decision" is, in contrast to an "individual decision." In an individual decision, the question is "What do I do?" In a joint decision, the question is, "What do we do?" In thinking of options for joint decisions, you're thinking of possible plans that two or more people could agree on, to respond to the choice point.

Which of the following is a joint decision?

A. Someone is not feeling good, and they have to decide whether to go to work anyway or stay home.
Or
B. A person is interested in giving a lot of the family's money to a charity, but the person's spouse worries that they may not have enough money in case they need to use it later.

126. Here are some general types of options you can think of for a joint decision choice point.

1. One of them could just do what the other wants.
2. They could figure out a compromise, where each of them gets a part of what they want.
3. They might think of an option that gives them both what they want.
4. They can take turns, where one gets their way for a while and the other gets their way for another while.
5. The first could do what the second wants in exchange for the second doing something else for the first.
6. One could do what the other wants in exchange for some money.
7. They could separate from each other in such a way that each can make their own decision.
8. They could use some random method, such as flipping a coin, to see which one of them gets their way.

9. They could let some other person or group, such as a judge, decide what is fair.
10. If there's a group of people deciding together, they could vote on what to do.

This is a list of

A. ways to solve a specific problem,
or
B. general strategies that might work for lots of different problems?

127. Now let's practice listing options for a specific joint decision. Suppose that some people have some time off. One wants to take a hike, and the other wants to go swimming. I'll use the list above to give me ideas. Here are some options:

1. The second person can just give in, and they go for a hike. Or the second gives in, and they go swimming.
2. They could take a short hike, followed by a short swim.
3. They could take a hike along a stream where they can swim to take a break from swimming. OR They could decide to get together with friends and play basketball, after they discover that both of them would rather do this than either hike or swim.
4. They could take a hike today, and when they get some time off tomorrow, they can go for a swim.

5. One of them could give in, in exchange for the other cooking dinner for both of them.
6. One could give in, in exchange for the other one paying them some money (a strange option in this circumstance, but possible).
7. They could each do what they prefer to do either on their own or with someone else.
8. They could flip a coin to see which activity they do.
9. They could ask someone else to decide what would be the best thing to do today, and go by what that person says. (Again, a little strange, but possible.)
10. If there are not just two people, but several, they could hold a vote.

This list represents

A. Applying the general strategies listed in the previous section to a specific joint choice point.
Or
B. Coming up with options for this specific choice point that don't have anything to do with the general strategies of the previous section.

128. Now let's look at another joint decision choice point, and apply the same 10 general strategies to it.

Here's the choice point: One person wants to host a dance party at their apartment. But the second person lives in the apartment below, and is worried that the noise will keep them awake.

Options:

1. The upstairs person could just not have the party. Or the downstairs person could just put up with the noise.
2. The upstairs person could make sure the music is a lot quieter than it would otherwise be, and that the dances people do don't involve a lot of hard clomping on the floor.
3. They could figure out a time for the dance party when the downstairs person isn't in the apartment. OR The upstairs person could figure out a different place to hold the party that's even better than their apartment.
4. If the person upstairs wanted to have a dance party every week, they could have it only every other week, and give the downstairs person silence in the weeks between.
5. The upstairs person could have the party in exchange for giving the downstairs person dance lessons and inviting them to all the parties.
6. The upstairs person could have the parties in exchange for paying the downstairs person a certain amount of money.
7. One of them could move to a different place where they wouldn't need to worry about what the other wanted.

8. They could flip a coin to see whether the party took place or not.
9. They could let the apartment manager decide.
10. All the people who live in the apartments could vote on what the policy is about parties.

The fact that we listed 10 general strategies earlier, and there are 10 options on this list, is

A. A coincidence,
or
B. A consequence of the fact that the author tried to make an option for this choice point that is a specific example of each of the 10 general strategies listed earlier.

4.7. Pros and cons exercise

129. Here's the seventh requirement for level 4.

Given an option for a choice that someone could make, generate at least 6 items for a list of advantages or disadvantages, taking turns with someone else.

This is also known as the Pros and Cons Exercise. When you are thinking of pros and cons, think: what are the possible results, the consequences, of doing this certain option? If something good might happen, that's an advantage, or pro. If something bad might happen, that's a disadvantage, or con.

Here's an example of the pros and cons exercise. The option someone considers is buying an exercise bike.

Pro: They could get good exercise without having to go outside when it's bad weather.

Pro: They could get a lot of exercise without paying money for a gym.

Con: They would have to spend money on it.

Con: If they had to put it together from parts, this would take up some time and energy.

Pro: It could be a lot of fun putting it together, kind of like building things with Legos.

Con: They could run out of motivation to use it and not get any benefit from it for that reason.

Con: It would take up space in their dwelling.

Pro: Exercising with it could help them be healthy, for example not get heart disease.

Pro: Exercising with it could help them not to be overweight.

Pro: Exercising with it could help them sleep better at night.

Pro: Taking a quick intense minute on it could help them stay energetic in the daytime.

Con: If it vibrated against the floor, it might disturb the person in the apartment downstairs.

Pro: Roommates or family members could also benefit from the advantages of it.

Con: It might get them out of the habit of doing exercises that don't require any equipment.

Pro: It might be easier on their joints than doing exercises that involve a lot of jumping around.

When listing pros and cons, if we consider the above to be a good example,

A. You should first do the pros, and then the cons.
Or
B. You can do pros and cons in any order, putting them on the list as you think of them.

Level 5

5.1. 12 thought exercise on your own

130. Here's the first requirement for Level 5.

Do the 12 thought exercise with a situation the tester gives you, all by yourself, without being prompted for the next thoughts.

There are lots of examples of this in various of our books, but it's OK to be repetitive, because this is such a useful exercise to be able to do. Here's one more example.

Situation: There has been an election of class officers at a school, and you have narrowly lost the election.

1. Awfulizing: This is really bad that I lost, particularly when I came so close to winning!
2. Getting down on yourself: Probably if I'd tried harder, I could have won; I was too lazy.
3. Blaming someone else: My opponent seems to be gloating over their victory in a way that really bugs me.
4. Not awfulizing: This isn't so bad. Lots of people supported me.
5. Not getting down on myself: I could have worked harder at this, but that would have taken away time from

other useful things I did, so I don't want to punish myself.
6. Not blaming someone else: How my opponent is acting now makes almost no difference regarding anything good that will happen to me in the future, so I'm going to choose not to worry about it.
7. Goal-setting: I want to come across as gracious and set a good model of how people should act.
8. Listing options and choosing: I could congratulate my opponent in some sort of public way, I could do so directly to the opponent, I could thank all the people who voted for me. I could turn my attention back to school work. I think I'll do all of those options!
9. Learning from the experience: I learned from this that it's not really a problem losing an election like this, that I'm not disgraced at all.
10. Celebrating luck: I'm lucky to have a supportive family to talk with about this.
11. Celebrating someone else's choice: I'm happy about every person who chose to vote for me, and also for the people who voted for the other person who are nice to me anyway.
12. I'm really glad I chose to react to this situation in a calm and mature way!

5.2. Four thought exercise

131. Here's the second requirement for Level 5.

Level 5

Do the 4 thought exercise with 2 provocations and 2 situations that someone could be afraid of.

The 4 thought exercise is like the 12 thought exercise, only shorter. Given a certain situation, you make up examples of:

1. Not awfulizing
2. Goal-setting
3. Listing options and choosing, and
4. Celebrating your own choice.

A provocation is a situation that could make someone angry. Here's an example of the 4 thought exercise with a provocation.

Situation: You're listening to an audio book, and you're in a very suspenseful part, but a parent tells you to turn it off and come to supper.

Not awfulizing: I wish I didn't have to pause here, but this isn't terrible. It's not as though I can't ever come back to this.
Goal setting: My goal is to use good psychological skills and make a choice that will make me happy and my family members happy.

Listing options and choosing: I can ask my parent if I can listen for just a couple more minutes so as to find out what happens next. I can relax my muscles to calm myself. I can just pause the story and come back to it later. I can think about what's happened so far in the story, and I can wonder what will happen next, so that when I come back, I'll enjoy finding out what happened even more. Or I could just pause the story and try not to even think about it, and get to the table as quickly as I can. I think I'll pause now and have fun making up my own guesses as to what's going to happen. Maybe I could let my family members guess too, if they want to.

Celebrating my own choice: Yay, I think I came up with something that will make me happy and make my family happy!

This was a situation where lots of practice with the four thought exercise was meant to help the person feel calm and cool rather than being so

A. scared,
or
B. angry?

132. Here's an example of the 4 thought exercise with a scary situation:

Situation: A teenager is interested in getting into a relationship with another person. The other person invites that teenager to smoke marijuana together. The teenager doesn't want to smoke marijuana, because of lots of knowledge about bad side effects, but is scared that the other person will reject them.

Not awfulizing: This isn't such a terrible situation—if the other person would reject me because of not smoking, then that's a signal that I can find other people more favorable to be in a relationship with.
Goal setting: I want to stick up for myself and be true to my self-care goals. I want to make a good decision about what type of relationship to have with this other person, if I have some sort of relationship.

Listing options and choosing: I could explain to the person right away that I've read about the effects of marijuana and I'm not interested in using it, ever. Or I could keep quiet about that. I could make a counteroffer —I could invite the person to take a walk with me outside. During that time, I could get to know more about the person. I could invite the person to have supper with me instead. I'm going to choose to just say, I'm not a marijuana smoker, but how would you like to take a walk with me instead? If the person says marijuana, take it or leave it, I'll leave it!

Celebrating my own choice: I'm really glad I made a choice to stick up for my own self-care!

What was the fear that the person would try to reduce by doing this example of the four thought exercise?

A. The fear of rejection by other people if the person didn't join in and conform to their behavior.
or
B. The fear of being harmed by the drug they were using, if the person used it.

5.3. Brainstorming options

133. Here's the third requirement for Level 5:

For 2 situations that the tester gives you, generate options by yourself, and come up with at least 4 of the options listed as reasonable ones for that situation.

Here's a sample situation: Someone has a problem that they tend to leave so much stuff lying around that they have a cluttered up room where things tend to get lost really easily, and there are lots of distractions.

This is a self-discipline choice point, and some of the options that we think of for this situation will probably help us for lots of other self-discipline choice points. Why don't you practice by thinking of all the options you can, on your own, and see if you can come up with at least four of the ones listed next. This is a fairly difficult situation, so don't feel bad if the options don't come, other than "Just clean it up."

The author now wants

A. the tutor and the student to take turns,
or
B. the student to practice listing options all by themselves?

134. Here are some options. See if at least four on this list are also on your list. If you are reading this aloud, I recommend you take turns reading the following list of options.

1. They could throw away everything in the room that they don't really want.
2. They could take the things they don't want that are worth something, and donate them to a charity that resells them.
3. They could get some boxes and take the things that aren't needed to some place where they can be stored.
4. They could put away the things that should stay in the room but can be gotten out of the way—for example books onto bookshelves, papers into filing cabinets, objects in their "homes."
5. They can break the big task down into separate parts, and try to feel good about completing each part.
6. They can try to congratulate themselves with their self-talk for every bit of progress they make.

7. They could make a regular time each day to work on organizing the things in the room.
8. They could write in their appointment calendar, appointments to organize the things in the room.
9. They could figure out some reward for themselves that they will get only when the room is uncluttered and neat.
10. They could get someone else to help them carry out the plan of rewarding themselves, to hold them accountable so they won't get the reward before they've earned it.
11. They could have some friend or family member be with them when they are organizing, so they can chat and have fun while doing the work.
12. They could take a "before" picture and send it to someone, so that they could have the pleasure of also sending the person an "after" picture when the room is uncluttered and neat.
13. They could make a written list of the reasons why they want to get the room uncluttered and neat, so as to increase their motivation.
14. They could listen to music that they like while doing the task, so they would enjoy it more.
15. They could read what people have written about organizing and decluttering, to get themselves psyched up for the task and get some tips on how to do it.
16. They could do fantasy rehearsals of doing the work on this task and feeling really good about it when they have made some progress.

17. They could give their room a rating each day and keep a table or graph to see how they do over time at meeting their goal.

How did you do? Did you think of at least 4 of the things on this list?

The author thinks that the main reason to work to be able to list lots of options like this is

A. Option-generating skill makes people happier because it helps them make better decisions.
or
B. Practicing listing options helps people get better grades when they write papers.

135. Now let's make a list of general ways that people can help themselves with self-discipline choice points. Some of these were on our previous list.

1. They can make an "internal sales pitch," or a written list of reasons why they want to accomplish the goal that takes self discipline, so they can be more motivated.
2. They can break the tasks down into little parts so they won't get overwhelmed by too big a job.
3. They can reward themselves with their self-talk for every bit of progress they make.
4. They can set up a regular routine for doing the self-disciplined activity.

5. They can write appointments with themselves in an appointment calendar, to do the job.
6. They can figure out a tangible reward for themselves for milestones of progress.
7. They can get someone else to help them get the reward only when they've earned it.
8. They could find someone to do the job with, so it will be more fun.
9. They can use music or something else to make the job more pleasant.
10. They can read what people have written about this, to psyche themselves up and get tips.
11. They can monitor their progress with daily ratings kept in a table or graph.
12. They can monitor their progress with pictures of before, during, and after.
13. They can do fantasy rehearsals of doing the job and feeling good about it.

These are some options that apply

A. to only one self-discipline choice point,
or
B. to many self-discipline choice points?

136. Now let's take another specific self-discipline choice point, and show how the general options we listed help us come up with good options. I'm just going

to use the same options just listed, only make them specific to the particular choice point.

The choice point is: someone tends to put off doing schoolwork tasks until the last moment. The person would like to do the work farther ahead of time.

1. They could make a written list of the reasons not to put off the work, and read that list often.
2. They can break big assignments down into little parts that aren't so overwhelming.
3. Each time they make progress, they can say to themselves, "Hooray, I made some good progress!"
4. They can get into the habit of doing the schoolwork at a routine time every day.
5. They can write deadlines for finishing various parts of big projects into their appointment book.
6. They can give themselves 5 potato chips, only when they check off one of the tasks on their to do list.
7. They can give the potato chips to another family member to keep, so that they have to report doing the work before getting them as the reward.
8. They can find a study buddy who is serious about working, to have work sessions with, either in person or connected electronically.
9. They can play soft classical music in the background if this makes it more pleasant to do the work and doesn't distract them.

10. They can read random parts of any book on how not to procrastinate, to psyche themselves up and get tips.
11. They can give themselves a grade from 0 to 10 each day, where 0 is total procrastination and 10 is no procrastination at all. They can make a table or a graph.
12. They can take pictures of grades or graded papers before and after this project.
13. They can fantasy rehearse getting to work at the appointed time without putting it off, and feeling really good about doing this.

To generate this list of options for self-discipline in schoolwork, the author

A. thought up a whole new set of ideas,
or
B. used the same ideas that were generated so as to apply to just about any self-discipline choice point?

5.4. Ways of reducing fear or aversion

137. Here's the fourth requirement for Level 5:

When the tester gives you a fear or aversion that someone might have, make up a way that they person could help themselves get over that aversion, in at least 7 of the following 9 ways.
1. estimating the danger,
2. taking it gradually (hierarchy),

3. staying in the scary situation long enough (prolonged exposure),
4. working on the skills of handling the situation,
5. relaxation,
6. choosing one's self-talk,
7. changing the pictures you make in your mind,
8. fantasy rehearsal, and
9. using “doing, not feeling” (behavior, rather than emotion) to judge success.

This is the same as in a previous requirement. It's repeated because reducing unwanted fear or aversion is so important for being happy and making other people happy. So here's another example:

Someone has a fear that other people think they look ugly or unattractive. They even have an aversion to looking at themselves because of the fear of ugliness.

1. Estimating the danger: Even if someone did think I was ugly, how bad would that be? I'm not some sort of ornament that is supposed to give them pleasure to look at. So I'm not in danger.

2. Taking it gradually (hierarchy) I'm going to try to get used to looking at myself in a mirror, starting out with looking at a small mirror from far away, and gradually working up to a big mirror closeby.

3. Staying in the scary situation long enough (prolonged exposure). Instead of avoiding people, I'm going to figure out a safe person or group to be with, and plan to be with them for long enough that I can get used to people's seeing me.

4. Working on skills that help handle the situation. I'm going to work toward helping people who in emergency medical situations. People who need emergency help don't care whether the person helping them is attractive or not, as long as they are nice and very competent.

If the person had used the strategy of working on getting very good at social conversation, so that people would enjoy talking with them, and the person could focus on that rather than how they looked, that would be an example of

A. estimating the danger
or
B. working on skills?

138. Now we continue with the example of thinking of 9 ways of reducing a fear or aversion. We're on the fifth way.

5. relaxation. I think about how I look, and at the same time, relax my muscles.

6. choosing one's self-talk. Here's what I want to say to myself: "Being attractive is not my chief goal. My chief goal is doing good things and being kind to people, and cultivating relationships with people who value those things."

7. changing the pictures you make in your mind. I am aware that I tend to imagine people looking at me and judging me on how I look, and I imagine those judgments wounding me like arrows. I want to practice imagining that I have a shield that will make any negative judgments from people bounce away as if I have a plexiglass shield around me.

8. fantasy rehearsal. I imagine myself being with people and interacting with them, thinking about all sorts of other things other than what they think about how I look. I imagine myself looking in the mirror and thinking, "You're the only body I've got; we have to have a friendly relationship, partner!"

9. using “doing, not feeling” (behavior, rather than emotion) to judge success. As I go to my emergency responder class, I plan to count this as a big success just from walking in and staying the course, even if I feel nervous and self-conscious the whole time!

If the person had imagined someone making insulting comments about how they looked, and the person practiced thinking, "Pleasing this person is not my job," and feeling apathetic about the person's comments, and saying "Whatever," that would have been an example of

A. relaxation,
or
B. fantasy rehearsal?

5.5. Tones of approval

139. Here's the fifth requirement for Level 5.

When your tester gives you different phrases to say, with one of three different degrees of approval and enthusiasm, be able to say them with the degree that the tester asks for. In other words, be able to say things with tones of voice that are either neutral, small to moderate approval, or large approval.

A neutral tone of voice sounds sort of like a robot is saying it. The word "monotone" means that the pitch of the voice doesn't change much—it stays close to one note.

Small to moderate approval sounds energetic, pleasant, and enthusiastic, but not extremely excited.

And large approval sounds very energetic, very enthusiastic, and very excited!

Here are some phrases that you and your tutor can practice with.

1. Wow, I like that.
2. How did you think of that?
3. I appreciate all the work you've done.
4. Good going.
5. I totally agree.
6. Can you believe it?
7. You did it.
8. Thanks for having this session with me.
9. Oh. Tell me more.
10. Oh my gosh.

Practice with the tutor saying these in different tones, with the student identifying whether the tone was neutral or small to moderate or large approval.

Then practice with the tutor telling the number of the phrase and asking for one of the three tones, and the student saying that phrase with that tone.

The purpose of this exercise is

A. for the tutor to hear some well deserved approval for all the work they have done,
or

B. for the student to get good at communicating different degrees of approval in the words they say?

140. Why is the tones of approval exercise important? Because when you are with someone, every time you open your mouth to speak, you are sending a signal about how you feel about whatever you're talking about. Sometimes you're also sending a signal about how you feel toward the person you're talking to! These signals are very important. Someone who is stuck in a neutral tone of voice, for example, has a harder time with relationships, because other people tend to get the feeling, "This person doesn't care about me or about what is going on," and they tend to look for someone who will send them some signals of being valued.

What point did this text unit make?

A. Being able to regulate your tones of approval and enthusiasm helps people to enjoy their relationships with you more.
or
B. Being able to regulate your tones of approval and enthusiasm will help a lot if you ever do any acting in plays or movies.

5.6. Greeting, parting, and PAPER in social conversation

141. Here's requirement 6 for Level 5.

Level 5

In social conversation, people often do greeting rituals at the beginning, parting rituals at the end, and in between, they talk about topics that can be remembered by the mnemonic PAPER. Tell why greeting and parting rituals are important. Give some examples of what people would say in greeting and parting rituals, and also tell the 5 topics that are remembered by PAPER.

Greeting and parting rituals are important because they let the other person know you care about them, that they make a difference to you, that you have a relationship with them, that you are not ignoring them. For greeting rituals you can say Hi, How are you, Good to see you, Hello, What's up, Hey. For parting rituals you can say Good bye, See you later, Take it easy, Farewell. With all these you can say the person's name.

The five topics that people often talk about are: Places in their lives (Where do you live? Where do you go to school?)

Activities (What do you like to do?),

People (Do you know ___? Do you have a brother or sister?),

Events (What are you going to be doing this week end? What's been happening in your life?) and

Reactions and ideas (What do you think about this:...? How did you feel about that? What do you want the most out of life? What are some of your views on ethics?)

This text unit might help solve which problem?

A. "I sound too much like a robot when I chat with people."
or
B. "I have trouble thinking of what to say when I talk with people."

5.7. Social conversation role play on your own.

142. Here's requirement 7 for Level 5.

Do the social conversation role-play, playing both parts yourself. Play two people having a social conversation in a situation the tester gives you. Have the two people:

1. Use some greeting and parting rituals.
2. Use the four ways of listening (reflections, facilitations, follow-up questions, positive feedback);
3. Take turns giving each other the floor often enough;
4. Model some tones of approval and enthusiasm.

If people can learn to do social conversations well, in ways that are pleasant for both people, they have a way of getting enjoyment, and giving other people enjoyment, that will last a lifetime! And if we think of the two important goals as being happy and helping others to be happy, that makes social conversation pretty important! Practicing social conversation playing both parts yourself is a great way to refine this crucial skill.

If someone either is almost completely silent during a social conversation, or talks almost the whole time without stopping, which of the four criteria above is the person missing out on?

A. Using some greeting and parting rituals.
or
B. Taking turns giving each other the floor often enough.

143. It's not easy playing both parts of a social conversation. It's very wise to practice before you do your test!

Here's an example of making up both parts of a social conversation. This is an imaginary conversation between a person named Sondi Smith and the ghost of Alexander the Great. If two people are reading this aloud, I recommend that one of you play the part of Sondi Smith and the other play the part of Alexander the Great.

Sondi says, "Hi, my name's Sondi Smith. What's your name, Mr. Ghost?"

Alexander says, "Hi Sondi. I'm the ghost of the Greek person named Alexander. The history books tend to call me Alexander the Great, but I don't think that what I did was so great."

Sondi says, "Oh? You don't feel very good about what you did when you were alive? Tell me more, please."

Alexander says, "Well, I went around fighting different groups of people and taking them over and making an empire. But the reason I had to have armies is that they didn't want to be taken over."

Sondi says, "So you took them over against their will, huh?"

Alexander says, "Yes, and probably lots of people got killed who wouldn't have if my armies and I had just left them alone."

Sondi says, "If I understand you right, since you've been a ghost, you've changed your mind about how great it is to conquer other people?"

Alexander says, "That's right, I've noticed what goes on in the world and I have become a big fan of nonviolence."

Sondi says, "Congratulations to you for keeping an open mind and thinking and learning!"

Alexander says, "Please tell me about yourself, Sondi."

Sondi says, "I'm in school studying how people can hold talks with leaders of nations, to help them from going to war."

Alexander says, "Wow, it sounds like you've chosen something very important to study."

Sondi says, "Alexander, I have to go now, but could we talk more later? Maybe you could share with me some ideas on how to have a peaceful world."

Alexander says, "That would be great, I would love to do that. Here's how you get in touch with me....."

Sondi says, "Thanks! Talk with you later, Alexander."

Alexander says, "Sounds good. See you later, Sondi."

In this conversation, Sondi used

A. more reflections than facilitations,
or
B. more facilitations than reflections?

5.8. Resistant, compliant, and goal-directed

144. Here's requirement 8 for level 5.

Explain three attitudes toward doing something: being resistant, compliant, or goal-directed. When you are given some examples of behaviors, tell which of these three the person's behavior is an example of.

The rest of this chapter explains the ideas of resistant, compliant, or goal-directed.

These words can apply to how people deal with challenges of trying to learn things, improve their skills, or make better habits. Let's first think about challenges where the goals are good ones to work at.

Here are some examples of the types of challenges we're talking about.

- Learning to program a computer.
- Acting kinder to people.
- Getting skilled in anger control.
- Learning touch-typing or keyboarding skills.

- Learning a school subject like chemistry, history, etc.
- Having better conversations with people.
- Getting into good physical shape.
- Becoming a better reader.
- Getting generally better in psychological skills.

All the things on the list are:

A. things you can get better at or learn in order to improve yourself or your skills.
or
B. different attitudes people can have toward learning new things.

145. This also has to do with attitudes toward doing work of any kind, not just work toward learning skills. For example:

- Working in a job.
- Doing schoolwork.
- Doing chores to help out the family or oneself.
- Doing maintenance tasks like cleaning up.
- Doing the work involved in maintaining relationships, for example writing thank you notes.

Which of the following two would be more similar to the examples we just gave?

A. Working to get better at the skills of calming oneself and relaxing.
or
B. Eating cotton candy when someone offers it to you at an amusement park?

146. Let's talk about three different ways that people can act when faced with a challenge like one of those we've listed.

The first way is to *resist* doing the activities that would accomplish something. If someone gives them some homework, they may put it off, or just refuse to do it. If someone gives them some advice, they may just tune it out, and not listen to it. If someone is holding a session with them to teach them, they may try to get the person to end the session as soon as possible. If there are phone sessions where they work on the skill, they may try not to go to the phone. If there are books that they use, they might try to lose those books on purpose. If someone tells them they have an appointment for a training session, they might groan and object. They might think, "How can I get out of doing this work?"

We can call this way of acting and thinking the *resistant* way.

What's a summary of this text unit?

A. Of three different attitudes toward learning new things, the third is best.
or
B. When people are mainly interested in getting out of doing the work necessary to learn or accomplish something, they are using the *resistant* style of acting and thinking.

147. The second way of acting, when faced with learning challenges, is to *comply* with a teacher or helper's requests or directions. When someone tells them it's time to work, they go ahead, even though they may not feel like it. If their teacher assigns homework, they try to do it. If someone asks them to read from a book, they read.

But if someone doesn't assign them to do some work, they are not likely to do the work on their own. They are not spending lots of energy thinking, "How can I get better at this?" Instead, they're just doing what they're told to do. They may be happier when they are assigned less work, and less happy when they have to do more work.

This way of thinking and acting is called the *compliant* way.

If there are two learners who are the same in the most important ways, except that one uses the resistant way and one uses the compliant way, which one of the two is more likely to succeed at learning the new skills?

A. The one with the resistant way.
or
B. The one with the compliant way.

148. Moving from the resistant to the compliant way of thinking and acting can be a hugely important step for a person. The compliant way allows a person to make all sorts of improvements and to learn all sorts of things that would be impossible with the resistant style.

But there's a third way of approaching learning new things, called the *goal-directed* way. Learners who use this approach are thinking, "I really want to get better at this. How can I accomplish this goal in the best way?" If these learners are taking a course that has a certain textbook, they might sit down and read the textbook even when they are not asked to. If there is a topic that isn't covered by their teacher, they might look up their own readings about the topic. They might buy or borrow other books on the subject. They might practice on their own to get better at the skill, even though no one is making them do it. If their tutor can't hold a session, instead of thinking "Yay, I have a holiday," they might think, "I'll do some work on my own!"

Someone wants to learn typing skills. The person buys a book on the subject, studies the exercises, and practices every day, until the person can type really fast and accurately. This person gives an example of the

A. compliant approach,
or
B. the goal-directed approach?

149. Some people never get to the stage of using the goal-directed approach to learning. They go to their jobs, and they do what their boss tells them to do. They come home and relax, by watching TV for example. They have fun however they can. They are not very interested in improving themselves. If they comply well, and if the person giving them directions tells them worthwhile things to do, they can be quite happy. The compliant style suits them.

The author's attitude is that for worthwhile goals, where a leader makes very good decisions about what work to assign,

A. One should never be satisfied with the compliant style by itself—to be truly fulfilled you must reach the stage of goal-direction.
or
B. The compliant style is lots better than the resistant style, and people using it can sometimes do OK.

150. Someone has a phone tutoring session scheduled at a certain time. He remembers the time, but his parent doesn't. The phone rings at that time, but his parent lets it ring, thinking it's a junk telemarketing call. The student thinks, "Yay, I'm going to get out of doing my work today."

The student in this example is using

A. the goal-directed style,
or
B. the resistant style?

151. Someone wants to get into good physical condition. The person makes a rule that the person will not watch TV without at the same time pedaling an exercise bike. The person follows that rule.

If someone else had made the rule and the person had followed it, that would have been an example of the compliant approach. But when people make rules for themselves that are meant to help them achieve something, and they follow their own rules, they are using

A. The goal-directed approach,
or
B. the resistant approach?

152. A student is asked to read a bunch of pages from a book and answer questions on the reading. But the student finds the answers on the Internet and is able to put the correct answers on the assignment without even doing the reading. The student is glad to have gotten out of the work of reading the book.

The student has a

A. resistant attitude,
or
B. goal-directed attitude?

153. A person wants to learn to program a computer in a certain language. The person knows that there are books and online training materials that would provide all the knowledge necessary. But the person knows himself well enough to know that he needs someone who is asking him to do the work. He knows that he needs to be accountable to someone. So he looks for a course, and signs up for the course, and does his homework in the course, and learns what he has set out to learn.

This person has a goal, and figures out the best way to achieve it. So the person is in some ways goal-directed. But at the same time, the person feels more comfortable learning when most of the time he can use

A. the resistant approach,
or

B. the compliant approach?

154. The last example illustrates that we don't always fall neatly into one category. We can feel really resistant on some days, and feel really goal oriented on others. We can feel compliant with some teachers, and resistant with others. We can feel goal-oriented on some tasks, and resistant on others.

Sharon's mom wants Sharon to play the piano really well. Sharon does not want to learn the piano, and has told her mom that, but her mom won't take no for an answer. Sharon is really interested in cross-country running. She goes out and runs on her own very often, and loves to see her times getting lower and lower. But if there is any way that Sharon can get out of practicing the piano, she finds that way.

It sounds from this as though

A. Sharon is a resistant person.
or
B. Sharon is generally goal-oriented for cross-country running, and resistant for piano playing.

155. People who are goal directed workers often use *self-assigned tasks*. These are tasks that no one tells them to do – they tell themselves to do these things, so they can meet their goal. Someone who wants to get more physically fit goes out running, even though no

one tells her to. Someone who wants to control his temper better does fantasy rehearsals of staying cool when people are rude. Someone who wants to be less scared practices relaxation methods every day, without anyone else making them do it. These are tasks that people assign to themselves. We see these as examples of "self-directed" behavior.

Which of the following is a self-assigned task, or self-directed behavior?

A. Some kids do push-ups and sit-ups as soon as they wake up each morning, because their camp counselor insists that they do this.
Or
B. Some kids stop eating between meals, because they want to lose weight, even though no one tells them they have to do this.

156. When someone asks Krinda, "What do you want to achieve or accomplish?" Krinda just gives the person a blank look, and replies, "I don't know." The person asks, "Do you have anything you want to work on, or things you want to get better at?" Krinda says, "No."

We would tend to guess that Krinda would NOT use which of the following attitudes?

A. compliant,

or
B. goal-directed?

157. A team of scientists worked to figure out what DNA is made of and how its building blocks are put together. One of them wrote that if there was some piece of knowledge that they didn't have, that they needed, they would just look it up. They would learn anything they needed to learn, that would help them figure out how the DNA molecule works. They were using the

A. goal-directed approach,
or
B. compliant approach?

158. Sondi feels unhappy and depressed. Sondi thinks, “I don’t want to stay this way. I want to make my life better.” Sondi looks and reads and asks to find out which are the best books that tell how not to be depressed and how to be happy. Then Sondi buys some of these and devotes some time every day to reading them and also to doing the exercises and tasks the books recommend. Sondi’s approach to mental health skills is

A. compliant,
or
B. goal-directed?

159. Leslo tries to teach himself to play the guitar. He buys some books and finds some good videos. But he finds that he just can't motivate himself to do the work. There are too many other things that he also wants to do. So he starts taking lessons. Now his teacher commands him to practice certain exercises. He obeys the teacher's commands, and he is very successful in learning to play the guitar. Once he gets fairly good at playing, he finds it much easier to practice and pick up new guitar skills on his own.

This story illustrates that

A. It's better to succeed using the compliant approach than not to succeed in a more self-directed way of learning.
Or
B. If you're not goal-directed enough to learn all on your own, you might as well give up on learning the skill.

160. So far we've been talking about work or learning or goals that are *good* to do. But not all things that people try to do, or try to get other people to do, are good! When we're talking about bad or wrong behaviors, usually the resistant approach is better to choose than either the compliant or goal-directed approach!

In the neighborhood where Teras lives, lots of kids are very goal-directed about learning to be good street fighters. They say to Teras, "Come on! Fight that guy! Show what you can do!" But Teras is not compliant with them. Teras avoids them and gets out of practicing fighting skills in any way he can. It turns out that by doing so, he successfully avoids getting hurt or killed and hurting anyone else.

In this example the author seems to think that

A. The resistant strategy was better because the goal was not a good one.
Or
B. Compliance is always better than resistance, and goal-direction is always better than compliance.

161. What makes a goal a good one? If accomplishing something makes you happier in the long run, and it also helps you make other people happier, it's a good goal.

Selena has a goal of being really good with words: being a very good reader and speaker and writer. Meeting this goal helps her enjoy talking with people more, helps her get better grades and a better job, helps her enjoy reading, and helps her learn how to help other people.

Maleka has a goal of seeing how much alcohol she can drink in the shortest possible time, so that she will be famous among her friends. This turns out to harm her health and to get her into accidents that harm other people.

Why does the author feel that Selena's goal was better than Maleka's?

A. Because large numbers of people agree that it is better.
Or
B. Because of good or bad effects on the person herself and on other people.

162. Thrista is on a cheerleading team. The cheerleading coach wants the cheerleaders to do a cheer which brings up gory images of violence toward the other team. Thrista thinks that doing this cheer is not right. So Thrista refuses to do it, and talks to the school principal about the situation, even though this makes the cheerleading coach very mad.

In this example, Thrista's approach to the particular cheer the coach was teaching, was

A. resistant, because the goal was judged to be a bad one,
or
B. compliant, because the goal was judged to be a good one?

163. Sometimes it's best to combine two approaches.

Jesna wants to be a really good violin player. So Jesna watches and listens to good players and tries to imitate them, reads about how to use good technique, practices exercises in recognizing little differences in pitch, works on songs that haven't been assigned, and so forth. But Jesna also works with a teacher, who assigns work, and Jesna does it. The teacher makes suggestions and gives directions, and Jesna follows them.

Jesna is combining the

A. goal-directed approach and the compliant approach.
or
B. resistant approach and the compliant approach.

164. The people who accomplish the most in life tend to be very goal-directed. This isn't very surprising: the more you try to accomplish things, the more likely you are to accomplish things! What isn't so obvious is that people who are goal-directed tend to enjoy making progress toward their goals; they tend to be happy. The people who are very resistant to working on good goals tend to be unhappy.

Sepla is a surgeon, who wants very much to become a better and better surgeon. Sepla reads, studies, goes to conferences, observes others, experiments, and feels really good when some sign comes of increased skill in surgery.

Quonset never has really gotten able to do much work. Quonset lives with her parents. When she gets bored, she relieves the boredom by playing video games and watching TV. The idea of working or going to more school is scary and aversive. Quonset also is not particularly interested in pursuing relationships or working toward other goals.

Knowing nothing other than these things, who does the author suggest is likely to be happier:

A. Sepla,
or
B. Quonset?

165. How do people get to be resistant, compliant, or goal-directed on certain tasks? This question probably has a complicated answer. But one simple answer to it is that a lot depends on people's *reinforcement history*. This means: how much have they gotten rewards or payoffs for acting resistant, acting compliant, or acting goal-directed? If someone learns to read by working with someone who celebrates their progress often, and gradually finds that reading is a great source of fun and pleasure, that person has gotten a big payoff for working toward the goal of reading. On the other hand, if the person has lots of trouble with reading, and finds it embarrassing to work on it, and has a teacher who gets mad at them, the person might find that resisting and

escaping the work on reading leads them to feel better, in the short run at least. The person might be reinforced for the resistant style.

The phrase reinforcement history means

A. How much you have been rewarded or punished for acting in a certain way.
or
B. How much the people you admire and want to imitate give you examples of acting a certain way.

166. If you want to become more goal directed, you may want to try rewarding or reinforcing yourself! If you ever do a self-assigned task that helps you get closer to a goal, you can say to yourself, "Hooray for me! I'm not only getting closer to my goal! I'm also helping myself to become more goal-directed, and that will help me be happier!" Just saying things like this to yourself (we call it celebrating your own choice) helps you feel good about acting in a goal-directed way.

In this text unit the author recommends:

A. That you try to be as kind as possible to the people you come into contact with.
or
B. That when you act in a goal-directed way, you celebrate your own choice and feel good about it.

Level 6

6.1. SOIL ADDLE for decisions

167. Here's the first requirement for Level 6.

Tell what SOIL ADDLE stands for, and make up an example of someone using each of these in the process of decision-making.

SOIL ADDLE is a mnemonic for: Situation, Objectives, Information, Listing options, Advantages and Disadvantages, Deciding, Doing, and Learning from Experience.

Let's imagine that someone is deciding what foreign language course to take in school.

Situation: The person realizes that this is an important choice point, because they probably will not want to take the time to learn two additional languages well. So it would be good to make a choice and stick with it. The person realizes that it will take many hours to learn the language well, so it's good to pick one that will be fun and useful to learn.

Objectives: The person thinks: My goals are to pick a language that will let me speak to lots of people, one that I like the sound of, one that isn't too difficult, and one I can use if I travel to places I'm interested in going to.

Information: The person reads about different languages on the Internet. (For example, they look up how many people speak various languages. They find out that English, Mandarin Chinese, Hindi, Spanish, French, and Arabic make up the top 6. They listen on Youtube to people speaking different languages. They look at maps of where in the world different languages are spoken. They look up ratings of how easy various languages are to learn. They find people estimating for example about 150 hours for Esperanto, 600 hours for Spanish and French, 750 hours for German, and 2200 hours for Japanese and Mandarin Chinese.)

Listing options: The person considers Esperanto, Spanish, French, German, and Mandarin Chinese.

Advantages and Disadvantages: The person thinks things like this: An advantage of Esperanto is that it's so regular that I don't have to spend so much time memorizing. Also I like the idea that it could be a second language for everyone. A disadvantage of it is that there's no country where most people speak it, and fairly few people speak it in the world. Also it's not offered at my school so I'd have to get special permission to take it online. An advantage of both Spanish and French is that I like the way they sound. I like that they are both easier than German and Mandarin Chinese. I like that there are lots of countries where Spanish is the main language. Also an advantage of Spanish is that lots of people in my own country speak it.

Deciding: The person decides to go with Spanish.

Doing: The person takes a course in Spanish.

Learning from the Experience: The person finds that the teacher who teaches Spanish at their school tends to give low grades. The person thinks, "Next time I may at least take that into account when choosing what to study." But otherwise, the person enjoys Spanish and thinks, "I learned that my decision process was pretty good."

6.2. Making up choice points

168. Here's the second requirement.

Make up 6 choice points that someone could use to practice listing options and choosing or doing the pros and cons exercise.

We are at a choice point almost every waking moment. A choice point is just a situation where we have to decide what to do. Here are some examples of choice points.

A person wants to get better at singing. The person is deciding how to go about doing this.

A person is going to bed, and is deciding whether to set an alarm for a certain time or just get up when they wake up.

A person wants to lose some weight. The person wants to generate options about how to do this.

A person is choosing strategies for losing weight. The person is deciding whether to have a "no eating between meals" rule for themselves.

A person is deciding what to do for a career.

A person is walking on a hiking trail, and they are deciding whether to keep going or to turn around and go back to the start.

A person is deciding what their highest priorities are for getting better at skills—that is, what skills to put on the list for practicing most often.

A writer has several things in mind to write, and is choosing which one to write next.

Someone is invited to smoke marijuana with someone else.

Someone is crossing the street, and they can either carefully look both ways, or just walk across without worrying about traffic. Is this a choice point?

A. Yes
or
B. No?

169. Why is it good to be able to list choice points? Because the first step in making a good decision is to realize that you have a decision to make!

There are lots of decisions that we make unconsciously, without even thinking about of them. For example: I have taken lots of breaths today, and I can choose whether to take another one or not. It's OK not to think about this decision, but just to do what comes naturally—in fact it's good that I don't waste my energy having to actually think to decide on each breath I take! Or: I'm walking, and I just took a step with my right foot. Which one should I use for the next step? It's great not to have to think to make this decision!

The author thinks that

A. You should think carefully about every choice point, or
B. For lots of choice points, just doing what comes naturally without consciously choosing works fine.

170. But for lots of other choice points, it's important to think carefully, and NOT to necessarily just "do what comes naturally." For example:

Someone is driving. The person notices a tendency to go faster and faster, and has to choose how fast to go.

Someone is eating. The person notices an urge to keep on eating many many calories, and has to choose whether or not to do this.

Someone can pick whether to have a standard bedtime, or whether to go to bed whenever they feel like it.

Someone gets the urge to scream at someone in anger, and they can choose whether to do this or not.

In all these examples, it may be very helpful for the person to think: "Wait! I'm in a choice point! I want to make a good one!"

Which of these two choice points do you think is better to really think about, as contrasted to doing what comes naturally?

A. Someone is lying down, and they can either keep lying on one side, or shift to the other.
or
B. Someone is in a program to learn psychological skills, and they can either continue it or discontinue it.

6.3. Types of kind acts

171. Here's requirement 3.

Be able to name at least 8 different types of kind acts, and tell a celebration or skill story illustrating at least two of them.

Level 6

Here are some types of kind acts. If two people are reading this aloud, I recommend you take turns reading aloud the things on the following list (and all lists of this sort).

1. Helping
2. Complimenting, congratulating
3. Expressing thanks
4. Being a good listener
5. Teaching, or learning from
6. Forgiving
7. Consoling (trying to comfort someone when they feel bad)
8. Spending time with, keeping company, inviting
9. Being cheerful, approving, funny, or fun-loving with someone
10. Being affectionate
11. Giving
12. Doing fun things with someone
13. Working together
14. Working to benefit someone else
15. Entertaining someone
16. Healing or relieving suffering
17. Working out disagreements rationally
18. Being assertive, not spoiling

What is the reason for getting very familiar with these types of kind acts? It's that one of our two big goals is making other people happy, and the list you just read gives 18 ways of accomplishing that goal! If you want to become a kinder person, a great way to do it is to make up fantasy rehearsals of doing each of those types of kind acts! Another way is to watch for opportunities to do these things, and try to celebrate and feel good when you are able to do one of them!

Suppose someone who has made a lot of money with a computer company contributes a lot of it to try to cure infectious diseases. Which of the types of kindness listed above do you think this is an example of?

A. Being a good listener and entertaining someone,
or
B. Giving and healing?

172. Why is "being assertive, not spoiling" on the list of kind acts? Because sometimes giving people what they want at the moment is not the thing that makes them happy in the long run. For example, a child has a tantrum and hits his parent when he is asked to quit watching TV. It the parent gives in to the child at that moment, the parent is not helping the child in the long run, because the child is being rewarded for bad behavior! Or if a family member is alcoholic, it may be kinder for their family members to have a daily search for any alcohol in the house and pour it down the sink.

This is an example of their being assertive rather than giving the person what they want in the short run.

The author thinks that the more important think about kind acts is that they

A. make someone happy in the long term,
or
B. give someone what they want right now?

6.4. Kindness and selfishness stories

173. Here's requirement 4.

Make up 5 stories to add to the "Kindness and Selfishness" chapter of Programmed Readings for Psychological Skills, in which 3 are examples of kindness and 2 are examples of selfishness.

Here's are some examples of how to do this.

Someone stays for a week end at someone else's little cottage by the lake. The person leaves dirty dishes in the sink.

A. Kindness,
or
B. Selfishness?

174. Someone stays for a week end at someone else's little cottage by the lake. The person thinks about writing a thank you message to the person, but never gets around to it.

A. Kindness,
or
B. Selfishness?

175. Someone keeps track of when their friends' birthdays are, and calls each of them up on their birthday to wish them a happy one.

A. Kindness,
or
B. Selfishness?

176. Someone wants to learn to sing better. The second person has studied and practiced singing a lot, and helps the first person learn the skill, being encouraging and supportive while doing it.

A. Kindness,
or
B. Selfishness?

177. Someone is very good at grammar. The second person says something like "between you and I" which is not grammatically correct. (It should be "between you

and me.") But the second person figures that the first person isn't wanting a grammar lesson now, or maybe ever. So the second person responds to what the person is trying to say and doesn't act on the urge to correct the grammar.

A. Kindness,
or
B. Selfishness?

178. It's usually not hard to say whether the person in these stories did an example of kindness or selfishness. But it's a different skill to make up little stories yourself. I recommend you practice it now. Take turns making up little examples of kindness or selfishness kind of like the examples you just read. Doing that, rather than an A or B question, is the challenge now.

6.5. Methods of relaxation

179. Here's requirement 5.

Tell how to carry out each of the following methods of relaxation or meditation. 1. Breathe and relax the muscles. 2. Mind-watching. 3. The loving kindness meditation (also known as the good will meditation). 4. Meditation with movement.

Here's how to do these.

Breathe and relax the muscles: You sit and close your eyes. You become aware of the rhythm of your breathing, without trying to speed it up or slow it down. Each time you breathe in, you get in mind a certain muscle or group of muscles in your body, and focus your attention upon it. When you breathe out, you try to let off any tension in those muscles—you let them get more limp, loose, and relaxed. If you notice that your mind has drifted off this procedure, you avoid "getting down on yourself," but just gently swing back into relaxing some muscles with each breath.

In the breathe and relax procedure,

A. When you breathe in, you purposely tense some muscles.
or
B. When you breathe in, you just get some muscles in mind that you are going to relax when you breathe out; you don't purposely tense them before relaxing them.

180. Here's how to do the mind-watching meditation. You sit and close your eyes. You let your mind do whatever it naturally tends to do. You just observe and notice what your experience is, without criticizing yourself for thinking any particular thing. If you notice that you have forgotten to observe what your mind is

doing, you gently swing back to observing, without "getting down on yourself" for having forgotten.

Someone says, "In the mind-watching meditation, you just save out part of your brain to observe and notice what the rest of it is doing." Do you think this person is

A. correct,
or
B. incorrect?

181. Here's how to do the loving kindness meditation, also known as the good will meditation. You get in mind about three good wishes, such as the following:

May___ become the best ___ can become.
May ____ give and receive kindness.
May ____ live in compassion and peace.

You wish each of these things for yourself. Then you pick someone else, and wish these things for that person. Then someone else, and someone else, and keep going. You don't restrict these good wishes to people you like or admire. If you notice you have gotten distracted onto something else, you don't get down on yourself about that, but gently swing back to going through the good wishes.

Metso is doing the loving kindness meditation. Metso notices that the thoughts have turned to a homework assignment that is due. Which of the following is closer to what the author would advise for Metso to use as self-talk?

A. Oh, I'm such a bad meditator!
or
B. Time to gently swing back into the three wishes for people.

182. Here's how to do the meditation with movement. You don't sit and close your eyes with this one. You pick a certain motion to do over and over. One I like the best is where I stand, push my hands together, bend at the knees while moving the hands down toward the floor, then straighten the legs while raising the hands overhead. I like to do the motion fairly slowly and smoothly.

When you do this, there are at least three choices. One is to focus the attention on the movement you are making and the sensations it produces in the body. The second is to let the attention go wherever it will, and to notice where it goes—in other words, to do the mind-watching meditation while doing the movement. A third is to let the mind do whatever it wants without even making any effort to notice what it is doing.

Which of the following do you think is an advantage of the meditation with movement?

A. Modern life makes people sit down too much, and the meditation with movement provides a break from sitting.
or
B. It can be done on a bus or airplane without drawing attention to yourself.

183. Perhaps the most important part of any of these meditation techniques is to use the "power of suggestion" with yourself, and expect or imagine that using the technique will induce a feeling of peacefulness or calm or good will, or refresh yourself and "recharge your batteries," or give you a feeling of connection to what is most important in life, or allow you an important break from stress and pressure. In other words, you use positive fantasy rehearsal to imagine the meditation having the desired effect upon yourself. But it's also very important to be patient, and not to expect that such a result will happen immediately or without a lot of practice.

The author, in this text unit, says that a very important part of meditation is

A. slowing down the heart rate and turning down the arousal level,

or
B. expecting or imagining the desired long-term effect of the meditation: feeling calmer, feeling refreshed, feeling good will, etc., but not being too impatient to get that effect.

6.6. Worthy goals

184. Here's requirement 6.

Tell of at least two “worthy goals” that a person could have, and explain why those goals meet the test of making the person happier or better off and/or making at least one other person happier or better off. Also, tell of at least two goals that a person could have, that might take up a lot of time without making anyone much happier or better off.

Here are some goals that I think are examples of "worthy goals," and why they can bring happiness to self or others.

Growing food that is nutritious and healthy—because food is something that everyone needs.

Doing work that heals people's sicknesses or injuries—because it's good for people to be healthy.

Level 6

Learning to be a good writer—because this lets you communicate ideas that will be helpful to other people.

Learning skills of anger control and conflict resolution—because people sooner or later have conflicts with each other, and these skills can help get the conflicts solved without harm to people's bodies or to their relationships.

Learning to type quickly and accurately—because this makes writing easier and faster.

Doing kind acts often, and feeling good about doing them—because this directly makes other people and yourself happier.

Getting lots of physical exercise—because this helps you be healthier, and to sleep better at night, and it improves the mood.

Increasing my work capacity—because this will help me achieve any other goal I set.

When the author speaks of the goal of increasing work capacity, what do you think he means?

A. The ability to get a lot of productive effort accomplished in a day, without getting too distracted or needing to goof off for too long.
or
B. The capacity to forgive another person when that person has criticized you unjustly.

185. Here are some goals or activities that I think are less worthy than the first set I mentioned, because they can absorb a lot of time without making anyone better off. Some of these make people worse off.

Someone tries to be the best at a shooter game.

Someone works hard at being skilled at mixed martial arts.

Someone wants to show that they are at the top of the "dominance hierarchy" or the "pecking order" of a group—that is, that they can for example criticize others without others criticizing them. Or that they can bully other without others bullying them.

Someone works on an advertising project to try to get people to buy a certain type of cigarettes.

Someone has a goal of owning a car (or clothes, or a house, etc.) that is so expensive that it will impress people and show people that they have lots of money to spend.

Someone has a goal of getting political power, despite the fact that the person doesn't know how to govern well once they get that power.

Someone tries to get as many people as possible to show that they are attracted to the person romantically.

The author thinks that these goals

A. don't take long to achieve, but usually create a lot of happiness,
or
B. Can take up a lot of time and effort, but don't create much happiness (or sometimes create unhappiness instead).

Level 7

7.1. Feeling word, situation, and thought

186. Here's the first requirement for Level 7:

Name at least 10 “feeling words.” For 4 of them, tell of a situation and a thought that would be consistent with that feeling.

Why is the ability to do this a great skill to have? It helps you to think more effectively about what's going on inside you, as well as what is happening to you. Words are an amazingly powerful tool. If you are able to think in words about what you are feeling, you will probably make better decisions about what to do.

The ability to recognize the types of thoughts that give rise to certain feelings lets you do something else really important: to influence your feelings by choosing your thoughts. For example, someone is interrupted in a video game and asked to come and eat supper with the family. If the person would rather feel grateful than angry, the person might choose a thought like, "How nice that they bought food for me and made supper for me and want my company at suppertime!" If for some reason the person wanted to feel angry, they would think something like, "Why do they have to interrupt me just at an exciting part!!!"

The author talks about a way of influencing your own feelings in this text unit. What is it?

A. Practicing relaxation techniques to turn down your level of arousal.
or
B. Choosing what you say to yourself, in ways that produce the feelings you want to have.

187. Here's a long list of feeling words. If you're reading this aloud with someone, I recommend you take turns, one person reading one feeling word, and one person reading the next.

Usually pleasant: accepted, appreciative, amused, awed, attracted, calm, cheerful, compassionate, curious, close, confident, contented, elated, excited, free, friendly, fun, glad, glowing, grateful, happy, hopeful, interested, jolly, joyful, lighthearted, liking, love, moved, playful, pleasant, pleased, proud, relaxed, relieved, satisfied, self-assured, serene, silly, slaphappy, sympathetic, tenderness, thankful, tickled, wonder

Usually unpleasant: afraid, angry, annoyed, ashamed, bewildered, bitter, bored, bothered, burdened, disdainful, drained, brokenhearted, confused, impatient, disappointed, disgusted, displeased, disturbed, embarrassed, envious, startled, fearful, frazzled, frightened, frustrated, guilty, harried, hate, hopeless, horrified, hurt, impatient, irritated, jealous, lonely, low, mad, mortified, pain, rage, regret, resentment, sad, scared, self-critical, shocked, terrified, threatened, tormented, troubled, uncomfortable, uneasy, unfriendly, unpleasant, upset, worried

Could be either: amazed, astonished, concerned, flabbergasted, indifferent, excited, pity, worn out, suspicious, stirred

Which emotion might someone prefer to feel, in the situation where someone in a very immature way is trying to provoke them by insulting them?

A. mortified,
or
B. indifferent?

188. Now let's give some examples of thinking up a situation and a thought that might give rise to a certain feeling. If you're reading this aloud together, I recommend taking turns, changing the reader with each new feeling word.

Feeling word: scared
Situation: The person is going to sing in front of a bunch of people.
Thought: What if I mess up, and sound bad, and everybody feels sorry for me or laughs at me?

Feeling word: angry
Situation: The person finds that someone has stolen their guitar.
Thought: I would like to punish that bad person who did this!

Feeling word: proud
Situation: The person has been teaching someone to read, and the student has read some words for the first time.
Thought: Yay, we're succeeding! I've made some good choices about how to do this!

Feeling word: grateful
Situation: Someone spent some time with me, helping me learn useful things.
Thought: It's good of that person to spend time helping me!

Feeling word: ashamed
Situation: Someone invited me to go for a walk with them, and I told them to leave me alone, in a rude tone, because I was doing a video game.
Thought: I shouldn't have done that. I acted like a spoiled brat.

Feeling word: fun

Situation: I'm singing with some other people, and it sounds good.
Thought: Yay! How nice it is to be able to do this and have it sound pleasing!

Feeling word: envious
Situation: My sibling wins another award for being best at something, when I've never won any awards.
Thought: I wish I could have people approving of me and celebrating my accomplishments like they do.

Feeling word: accepted
Situation: I'm with a group of people, and they all seem to like me.
Thought: I'm really glad to be with a group of people who like me and consider me part of their group!

Feeling word: sad
Situation: I hear about someone who died in the pandemic.
Thought: That's too bad that they had to die. This will make their friends and family members very unhappy.

Feeling word: impatient
Situation: Someone is talking to me, and they keep talking on and on without stopping for a long time.
Thought: I wish they would hurry up and finish! If they don't stop soon, I'll interrupt them.

Level 7

Feeling word: interested
Situation: I'm reading a book about how the universe works, and it's telling me a bunch of cool things.
Thought: Wow, this is fun stuff to find out about! I want to find out more!

Feeling word: startled
Situation: I'm brushing my teeth, and a family member says hi to me from close by. I didn't hear or see them coming.
Thought: Whoa! What's that!

Feeling word: compassionate
Situation: I see at school someone being teased and picked on by some other people.
Thought: I bet that person feels bad; I want to make them feel better.

Feeling word: rage
Situation: I see at school someone being teased and picked on by some other people.
Thought: Why do they have to be cruel like that! They should be punished severely!

Feeling word: lonely
Situation: I have a day to spend all by myself.
Thought: I wish I could be with someone. I have no one to talk to.

Feeling word: free
Situation: I have a day to spend all by myself.
Thought; Hooray, I get to choose what to do. There are all sorts of fun things I can do by myself today!

Feeling word: drained
Situation: It's been a long and hard school day, and I've done lots of homework, and there is more to do.
Thought: I'm so tired of using self-discipline. I wish I could just relax or do something fun.

Feeling word: disgusted
Situation: I see a big group of people demonstrating to support a cause that I think it racist, immoral, and bad.
Thought: What a bunch of deplorable people. They give me the creeps.

Feeling word: stirred
Situation: I see a big group of people demonstrating to support a cause that I think is good and right and decent.
Thought: Yay, isn't it wonderful to see such a great cause being supported!

Now I recommend that you take turns thinking of more examples like this! You can use the same feeling words that have already been used, if you want. It would be possible to think of thousands of situations that could give rise to any feeling!

7.2. Ida CRAFt options for provocations

189. Here's requirement 2 for Level 7.

Tell the Ida CRAFt options for responding to provocations, and give an example of each of these with a provocation you are given.

A provocation is any situation that could make you angry. Provocations are very important situations to be able to handle well. In handling any situation well, it's good to be able to think of lots of options. Ida CRAFt is a mnemonic that helps you brainstorm options for provocations. Ida CRAFt is a mnemonic for:

Ignoring
Differential reinforcement
Assertion
Conflict-resolution protocol (Dr. L.W. Aap)
Criticism responses (T Paarisec)
Relaxation
Rule of law
Apologizing
Away from the other person
Friendliness
Force (nonviolent)
Tones of voice.

The list above is given so that

A. You can do all of them whenever you get a provocation,
or
B. You can think of more options to pick from when you get a provocation.

190. Here's a sample provocation. Someone is trying to study for a big test, but their younger sibling keeps on interrupting them, and saying, "Come on, do something with me. You're no fun." Let's let Ida CRAFt help us think of options.

Ignoring: They could just focus on the studying and not respond.

Differential reinforcement: They could ignore the interruptions, and later when taking a break, if the sibling has left them alone, they could do something fun with the sibling for a while, to reward the sibling for that.

Assertion: They could say, "I have an important test tomorrow, so I want you to please not interrupt my concentration."

Conflict-resolution: They could say: "You want to have fun together, and I appreciate that, but I have an important test I have to study for. Could we talk about this problem?"

Criticism responses: They could say, "You're right, unfortunately I'm no fun for now, because I have to study."

Relaxation: They could relax the muscles to help them respond calmly.

Rule of law: They could go to a parent and request that the parent use their authority to help them to be left uninterrupted.

Apologizing: They could say, "I apologize for not being able to play with you."

Away from the situation: They could go over to a friend's house or to a library to study.

Friendliness: They could say, "I'm glad you like to do things with me. I really wish I could."

Force: They could gently escort the sibling out of the room and lock the door.

Tones of voice: They could speak in a soft and low voice to avoid making the other person excited.

The phrase "differential reinforcement" means that

A. You reward the person for a certain behavior and don't reward certain other behavior.
or
B. You speak in calm and gentle tones of voice with the other person.

7.3. Catharsis theory versus rehearsal theory

191. Here's requirement 3 for Level 7:

Tell what the "catharsis theory" of anger is. Tell what science has to say about whether it's right or not. What's a different theory? What harm can the catharsis theory do?

Answer:

The catharsis theory is that when you yell angrily or hit a pillow or punch a punching bag or play a violent video game, you get your anger and aggression out of your system so that you don't feel angry any more.

Many experiments and studies tell us this theory is not right. For example, an experimenter randomly gave preschool children aggressive toys (weapons) or non-aggressive toys (boats and trains) to play with. Their dramatic play was more violent with the aggressive toys. If the catharsis theory were true, they would get the urge to be aggressive out by the dramatic play. But instead, the children who were more aggressive in their fantasy play were also more aggressive in real life, soon afterwards.

A different theory, which is consistent with scientific evidence, is the "rehearsal" theory. This is that when you act angry or aggressive, you are rehearsing acting angry and aggressive again. The practice can generalize to other situations or other aggressive behaviors. On the other hand, the more you rehearse acting in a calm and rational way to situations that might make people angry, the better you get at responding this way.

Which is closer to the author's attitude?

A. Both the catharsis theory and the rehearsal theory have their good parts, and both are right in several ways.
or
B. The rehearsal theory is correct and the catharsis theory is incorrect.

192. Scientists have surveyed families to find out how much they yell at each other in anger and how much they hit each other. If the catharsis theory were true, you would expect that family members who yelled more would get their aggressive urges out, and hit less. But just the opposite is found: those who yell more, also hit more.

If you feel joy, and you get together with people and laugh and have fun, do you get all the joy out of your system and feel depressed afterwards? Or if you feel loving, and you act in a kind and caring way to someone, do you get all those positive feelings out of your system and hate the person afterwards? Not usually! Usually it's just the opposite, as the rehearsal hypothesis would predict. If getting an emotion out of your system doesn't work with these emotions, there's little reason to think that anger should be an exception.

The catharsis theory can be harmful because it can get people practicing aggressive acts, thinking they are helping their anger control, when actually they are making it worse. Once a little boy hit someone without a reason. When someone asked him why, he said, "Because I didn't have my pillow handy." He thought that he needed to get his anger out somehow or other. The catharsis theory can lead people to act hostile, in very unwise ways.

The author thinks that when learning anger control, it is more important to

A. practice handling situations that could cause anger in a wise and reasonable way,
or
B. express your anger so as to get it out in ways that are not harmful to others, because otherwise it will build up until you "explode"?

7.4. STEBC fantasy rehearsals

193. Here's requirement 4.

Level 7

Take turns making up STEBC fantasy rehearsals of good responses to situations, doing at least 2 STEBC fantasy rehearsals yourself.

In a fantasy rehearsal, you imagine yourself handling a situation in just the way that you'd like to. In a coping fantasy rehearsal, you imagine that the situation is hard for you, but you triumph in handling it well. In a mastery fantasy rehearsal, you imagine that you have gotten to be a real master of this sort of situation, and handle it well with ease.

STEBC stands for situation, thoughts, emotions, behaviors, and celebration. You don't necessarily have to do these in order.

If someone does a fantasy rehearsal and imagines themselves feeling peaceful and serene in the situation, they are rehearsing a

A. thought,
or
B. emotion?

194. Here's an example of a coping fantasy rehearsal.

Situation: I go to a party, where I don't know anybody.

Thoughts: This is the sort of situation that has made me really anxious in the past. If I can have a triumph this time, that will be a big achievement. A triumph will be just hanging in here and acting reasonable and decent, and not necessarily impressing everybody, or even anybody. I remind myself that people have better things to do than to judge me, and that even if people make judgments about me that are bad, that's not a tragedy—I don't need for these people to become my fans. I want to try to have good conversations if possible but not worry about it if it doesn't happen.

Emotions: I feel nervous, but I also feel secure when I think that nothing awful is going to happen. I feel determined to make what I define as a success out of this.

Behaviors: I make eye contact with people and smile. If someone says something to me, I try to respond with a tone of some enthusiasm and approval. I do greeting rituals and introductions. I ask and tell people about the PAPER subjects (places, activities, people, events, reactions and ideas in our lives). I listen with four responses (reflections, facilitations, follow-up questions, positive feedback). If there are silences in the conversation, I don't worry about them.

Celebration: Hooray! I have had a major triumph! This is a courage skill and friendship-building skill triumph!

This is a fantasy rehearsal someone might use in getting over

A. A fear of socializing with unfamiliar people,
or
B. An aversion to being in closed spaces?

195. Here's an example of a mastery fantasy rehearsal. The person is working on an aversion to getting started on homework or school projects.

Situation: I have written down in my schedule an appointment with myself to start working on my homework at this time.

Thoughts: This is no problem. I'll do the work now, and then I'll feel good later about having it done. I'm going to look for any part of the work I'm doing that is interesting or fun or useful.

Emotions: I feel curious about the work I'm going to do. I feel good about myself for getting going on this without procrastination. I have a nice liberated feeling, not to feel any resistance to getting started.

Behaviors: I get started right way. I figure out what order I'm going to do the assignments in. I get going on the first one. I congratulate myself for every step that I complete. I look for the interesting, fun, or useful, and I find it. I go until the time I'd planned to take a break, and take a break for the planned amount of time, and then I get back to work! I keep going like this till I finish!

Celebration: Yay! I did this efficiently, without putting it off! Now I have some free time for the rest of the evening to relax and do other things! I also strengthened a really good habit!

In this fantasy rehearsal, the person is practicing

A. the way they think they probably would feel in the situation, as of now,
or
B. the way they would like to feel in the situation, in the future?

7.5. Dr. L.W. Aap on your own

196. Here's requirement 5 for Level 7:

Do a Dr. L.W. Aap role-play with a conflict or joint decision the tester gives you, playing both parts yourself.

You have probably read lots of examples of the joint decision role play, also known as conflict resolution role play, also known as Dr. L.W. Aap. In this challenge, you play both parts yourself. Here's an example of what you would do.

The first person (a parent) says: Could I talk with you about a problem? ... It's that when I tell you it's time for bedtime, you tend to either ignore me or to tell why you need to keep doing what you're doing. But if I leave it up to you when to go to bed, you usually stay up so late that it's hard for you to get out of bed in the morning.

The second person (their teenaged child) says: So you feel like I'm noncompliant when you tell me to go to bed, but if you just leave it to me, I stay up too late.

The first person says: That's right.

The second person says: My point of view is that I should be old enough to decide when to go to bed on my own. But I do admit that sometimes I just don't use the self-discipline to go to bed early enough.

The first person says: So you'd like to be in charge of your own bedtime, but you agree that sometimes you stay up later than is good for you.

The second person says: That's right. Want to list some options?

The first person says: I could just resign from having anything to do with your going to bed or getting up. If you stay up too late or don't get out of bed in the morning in time for school, that would be your problem, by this option.

The second person says: We could figure out a time for me to start getting ready for bed, and you remind me only if that time has passed.

The first person says: I could keep on reminding you when to go to bed and when to get up in the morning, and you could work on just being more compliant and polite.

The second person says: I could set an alarm that tells me when to get ready for bed, and set one of those lights that comes on to wake me up. You could congratulate me for responding to those rather than prompt me before I've gone to bed or gotten up.

The first person says: I think we've got some good ones. Want to talk about pros and cons?

The second person says: Yes. The main con of my just working on being more compliant and polite is that I'm already in a pretty bad habit.

The first person says: The pro of my just staying out of it altogether is that you get independence and I don't need to mess with it. The con is that we don't want to deal with the problem of your being late to school a lot.

The second person says: The pro of my responding to an alarm and a wake-up light, and your congratulating me some of the time for doing that, is that it gives me some independence, but it makes pleasant talk go on between us rather than unpleasant talk.

The first person says: I like that one. Want to give it a try first?

The second person says: Yes. Let's give it a try for a week and talk with each other again and see how it's gone.

The first person says: Sounds good. Thanks for talking with me about this.

The second person says: Thank you for discussing it with me!

The author probably believes that

A. Dr. L.W. Aap conversations are probably how most people in the world respond to conflicts.
or

B. If almost everyone practiced lots of Dr. L.W. Aap conversations through role playing, people would probably on the average be better at handling conflict than they are at present.

7.6. Ten methods of influence

197. Here's the sixth requirement for Level 7:

Tell what the 10 methods of influence are. When you hear some stories that give examples of these, tell what method of influence is being used.

What do we mean by a "method of influence?" We mean something that helps someone learn, change, do something differently, grow, get better at something, get worse at something—the reasons why people do what they do. If you want to help someone else do something, these are methods you can use. If you want to achieve a certain goal yourself, these are methods to help yourself do it.

These methods of influence can be used for anything from playing a piano to shooting a gun. But in this manual, what do you think we are particularly interested in using them to improve? The answer is: psychological skills!

A summary of this section is that

Level 7

A. People call other people "influencers" when they have lots of power to cause changes in the way other people think, feel, or behave.
or
B. There are 10 methods of influence that explain why people do what they do, that are particularly relevant to the question, how do people improve their psychological skills.

198. Let's list the 10 methods of influence.

1. Objective-formation
2. Hierarchy
3. Relationship
4. Attribution
5. Modeling
6. Practice
7. Reinforcement and punishment
8. Instruction
9. Stimulus control
10. Monitoring

If you take the first letter of each of these, in the order given, you get 3 words that help you remember the 10 methods of influence. Those 3 words are

1. OH RAM PRISM
or
2. LET'S GO SWIMMING

199. Now let's think about what each of these means. The first is objective-formation, also known as goal-setting. This refers to someone's becoming convinced that a certain skill is a good one to have, or that a certain habit is worth cultivating. As an example, it's harder to teach someone the skill of respectful talk if they think that respectful talk is for wimps and that insulting talk is the only way to get things done. It's easier for someone to cultivate the skill of kindness if they believe that being a kind person is one of the most important goals that can be achieved.

The second is hierarchy. This means that there are usually steps toward a skill or goal, that can be arranged in order of difficulty. (A list arranged in order is called a hierarchy.) It's good to work at the level that is not too hard, not too easy, but just the right level on the hierarchy of difficulty. That way you are not bored, not frustrated, but have a sense that you can succeed if you try hard enough.

The third is relationship. If you have a good relationship with the person teaching you, that helps. It is also possible to think of your relationship with yourself—the part of you that is working on something needs to have a good relationship with the part of you that is assigning work to you. A good relationship with the self means you are saying encouraging things to yourself, being honest with yourself about your mistakes, celebrating your accomplishments, and otherwise using self-talk well.

A tutor is working with a student on math. The tutor gives some tests to see what the student knows already. The tutor starts working just at the highest level where the student can be successful and can enjoy the work, no higher and no lower. The tutor is using

A. hierarchy
or
B. objective-formation

200. The next method of influence is attribution. If you think, "I can handle tough things that come my way," you are attributing to yourself the trait of fortitude. If you think, "That person isn't smart enough to learn that," you are making an attribution about that person, that the person can't learn the skill.

Do you attribute to yourself the capacity to achieve a goal, given enough work at it? Or do you attribute to yourself some fixed trait that can't be changed? The ways people talk about themselves and others tend to create attributions. Saying, "This is just the way I am, I'm super shy, I'll always be like this," does not attribute to oneself the ability to change. Saying, "There are several different things to learn, to get comfortable with social conversations with people.

They take a lot of work and practice, but I can learn them, and when I do, my life will be happier," attributes to oneself the ability to change. It's easier to get better at something if you believe that it's possible!

The fifth method of influence is modeling. We tend to imitate the examples of thought, feeling, and behavior that we see. Thus it's good to have models in mind of positive psychological skills.

The sixth method is practice. The more we carry out a certain chain of behaviors, the easier it gets to do them. Practice in fantasy does similar things to real-life practice.

Someone is going to give a speech. The person reads the speech silently, imagining themselves in front of the audience, imagining saying the sentences with expression. The person is using

A. practice
or
B. attribution?

201. The seventh method is reinforcement and punishment -- the consequences that occur after the behavior. Some of those consequences make a repeat of the behavior more likely, and some of those make a repeat less likely.

The eighth method is instruction. The person reads or hears an explanation of how to do the skill.

The ninth method is called stimulus control. This means that the person gets into a situation that tends to bring out the behavior in question. Someone wants to get more exercise, so they join a swimming team. Someone wants to stop drinking alcohol, so they get rid of any alcoholic drinks in the house. Someone wants to stop wasting so much time on watching TV, so they keep the remote for the TV where you have to walk upstairs to get to it.

The tenth method is monitoring. This means keeping track of how well the skill is being carried out or how much the goal is being met. Someone is trying to stop pulling at their hair, and they click a little counter each time they touch their hair. If the number is less than it was before, they celebrate, and they try to figure out how they did it. This is and example of monitoring.

A tutor is helping a student learn to read. Each time the student does a good job of sounding and blending a word, the tutor says something positive or complimentary that the tutor hopes will reward the student for persisting. The tutor is using

A. stimulus control

or
B. reinforcement?

202. Let's now practice identifying what method of influence people are using.

Someone wants to get better at all psychological skills. The person finds a book with examples of people doing psychologically skillful things, and the person reads those examples many times. The person is using

A. modeling
or
B. hierarchy

203. A person says, "I just feel nervous and uncomfortable when I have to socialize with someone I don't already know well. I've always been that way. I think that's just the way I am."

A second person says, "Have you ever studied anything that has been written on the art of social conversation? Like, for example, different topics that people frequently talk about? Ways of listening when someone else talks with you? How to communicate approval and enthusiasm in your voice?"

The first person says, "No, I never thought of that." So the first person starts reading about how to enjoy social conversation and help other people to do so.

The first person is taking advantage of

A. instruction
or
B. monitoring?

204. The same person we just spoke of starts to think, "Feeling uncomfortable in social conversations is not the way I always have to be. I can change by working at it, and learning. When I get skilled at having chats with other people, my life is going to be better." The person is now thinking of themselves as able to change rather than having to stay the way they are now. The person is using the power of

A. stimulus control,
or
B. attribution?

205. The person spends time just imagining pleasant and interesting conversations, to get into positive habits. The person also spends time having conversations with relatives, partly to be kind to them, but also partly to rehearse good ways of talking with people. The person is using

A. practice,
or
B. objective formation?

206. The person starts practicing conversations with people they feel very comfortable with. Then they practice with people they don't know quite so well. Then the person practices with people they don't know at all, but where they probably won't see the person again. Gradually the person works the way up to having social conversations with someone they don't know well, but would really like to get to know better. They have gone from the easiest situation to the most difficult. The sequence of steps the person goes through is called

A. a hierarchy,
or
B. an attribution?

207. Someone wants to keep from losing their temper so often. The person writes a list of reasons that they want to get better at anger control, and the person reviews that list daily. The person also writes, "Here's what I will be doing differently when I'm expert at anger control," and writes down very specifically what they want to be doing. The person makes a point of saying to themselves, at least once a day, "I wish that I will become very expert at keeping calm and cool even when I am provoked."

The person is using the power of

A. objective formation
or

B. monitoring?

208. The person who wants to get better at anger control finds a book with lots of conflicts, provocations, and criticisms listed in it. The person makes up a calm, rational, and reasonable way of responding to each of these situations, and imagines themselves doing these desirable ways of acting many times. The person is using fantasy rehearsal, which in our list of methods of influence is a way of

A. practice
or
B. attribution?

209. The person who wants to get better at anger control keeps a record of two types of events. The first is called "Times I lost my temper in an unwanted way." The second is called "Times I dealt with a provocation in a desirable way." The person tries to make the additions to the first list become less frequent, and the additions to the second, more frequent. As the person looks back over their records, they feel good about their progress. The person is using

A. stimulus control,
or
B. monitoring?

210. Someone is trying to do some writing, but the person gets tempted to get on the Internet and waste time. The person gets an old computer that doesn't connect to the Internet, and sets up a place to do writing using this computer. The person finds it easier to stay on task, because of their use of

A. reinforcement,
or
B. stimulus control?

211. A person has a sibling who sometimes says mean things to them. The person has been in the habit of responding to the sibling by arguing or protesting or defending. But the person decides that all these actions just reward the sibling for being mean. So the person decides that when the sibling says something mean, they will respond by just giving a blank look. But when the sibling is nice, the person will try to generate some excitement and enthusiasm that will be rewarding for the sibling. Over time, the sibling acts nicer, because of the person's skillful use of

A. reinforcement,
or
B. instruction?

212. Someone likes to play a game on the computer, but playing the game gets in the way of doing work. So the

person makes a plan to be able to play the game only after a certain amount of work has been completed. The game will be the reward for doing the work. The person uses great self-discipline to stick to this plan, and finds that they are able to get a lot more work done. The person has used

A. attribution,
or
B. reinforcement?

213. Someone is trying to do better at schoolwork. The person realizes that they criticize themselves very frequently and say encouraging and rewarding things to themselves very seldom. They read a book called *How to Be Your Own Best Friend.* They decide that they need to make their self-talk more friendly and kind. When they do, they get lots more work done. They have cultivated a better ____ with themselves.

A. relationship
or
B. stimulus control

214. Someone is in the habit of being too impulsive -- acting without thinking first. The person spends lots of time playing video games where you have to react very quickly to something you see appearing on the screen. The person decides to shift to playing chess. When the

person impulsively moves without thinking about the consequences, they tend to lose the game. When they think carefully about the options and what the consequences will be, they tend to win more. The person finds themselves getting more into the habit of thinking before acting. The person says, "Playing the new game helped me to ____ thinking before acting, and also gave me _____ when I thought carefully."

A. practice; reinforcement
or
B. attribution; stimulus control

Level 8

8.1. Emotional climate, CCCT, and REFFF

215. Here's the first requirement for Level 8.

Tell what is meant by the "emotional climate." Tell what CCCT and REFFF stand for, and what effects they have on the emotional climate.

In a good emotional climate, people enjoy each other, have fun with, like, love, help, approve of, get along well with, and find it pleasant to be with one another. The opposite situation is a bad emotional climate. A pair of people in any kind of relationship can have an emotional climate, as can any group of people or a family. The emotional climate can change, sometimes rapidly. Living in a good emotional climate is good for their mental health.

CCCT refers to commands, criticisms, contradictions, and threats. Here's an example of each: Command: Stop doing that. Criticism: You're not doing that right. Contradiction: You're wrong about that. Here's the right idea instead. Threat: If you keep doing that, you'll get punished. These are all useful at times, but too high doses of them are toxic to the emotional climate.

REFFF refers to the 4 ways of listening, plus telling about your own Experience: **R**eflections, telling about your own **E**xperience, **F**acilitations, **F**ollow-up questions, positive **F**eedback. These, plus a lot of helping, doing activities that are fun for both, having a good sense of humor, and using tones of approval, contribute to a positive emotional climate.

One of the points this text unit makes is that

A. Good emotional climates tend to make people mentally healthier.
or
B. Sometimes it's better to end a relationship than to continue to tolerate a very negative emotional climate.

8.2. T PAARISEC for response to criticism

216. Here's the second requirement for Level 8

Tell the T. Paarisec options for responding to criticism, and give an example of each of these with a criticism you are given.

Ida Craft is a mnemonic for options with any type of provocation. T Paarisec is meant to help you think of options for a particular type of provocation: being criticized. T Paarisec is a mnemonic for:

Thank you
Planning to ponder or problem-solve
Agreeing with part of criticism
Asking for more specific criticism
Reflection
I want or I feel statement
Silent eye contact
Explaining the reason
Criticizing the critic.

Suppose someone says, "You're a bad person!" and the second person says, "There have been times when I haven't done the best thing, I admit it." The second person is refusing to get defensive, and thus avoids giving the other person the power to judge them. This type of response to criticism is called

Level 8

A. Explaining the reason
or
B. Agreeing with part of criticism

217. Suppose the situation is that a first person shows a second person their math homework. The second person says, "This is too sloppy. You can't just write the numbers any old place -- you've got to line them up right! You'll be a loser in math if you keep doing it like this!" Let's let T Paarisec help us think of options for how to respond.

Thank you: Hmm. Keeping that in mind will probably help me. Thank you.
Planning to ponder or problem-solve: OK, let me do some pondering about that.
Agreeing with part of criticism: It's not the neatest work in the world, that's for sure.
Asking for more specific criticism: Could you say more about how to line them up right?
Reflection: So if I understand you, you think I should make it a high priority to write the numbers much more neatly.
I want statement: I still want to see if I got the answers right.
Silent eye contact: The person looks at the other person and just nods.
Explaining the reason: I tend to focus on getting the answers right rather than making it look good.

Criticizing the critic: I think you make a good point, but I wish you would come across as less insulting, for example by not using the words sloppy and loser.

Which two of these responses tend to be what most people naturally do in response to criticism: defend themselves, and attack the other person?

A. Explaining the reason and criticizing the critic,
or
B. Reflection and asking for more specific criticism?

218. A critic says, "You keep forgetting things! There must be something wrong with your brain!"

The other person responds: "Can you give me some examples of what you're referring to?"

This would be:

A. asking for more specific criticism
or
B. criticizing the critic?

219. Suppose that in response to the same criticism about forgetting, the person had said, "You think I forget things so much that there must be some medical reason; do I understand correctly?"

This would be

A. an "I want" statement,
or
B. a reflection?

220. Suppose that in response to the same criticism, the person had said, "Hmm. I'll have to think about that, and see what I notice." This is

A. Agreeing with part of criticism,
or
B. Planning to ponder or problem-solve?

221. Suppose that in response to the same criticism, the person had said, "Well, I do forget things sometimes, that's for sure." This is

A. Agreeing with part of criticism,
or
B. Thank you?

8.3. Exposures that increase or decrease fear

222. Here's the third requirement for level 8.

Suppose that someone is wanting to get over a fear. Suppose the person gets into the scary situation, but when the fear rises to a very uncomfortable level, the person escapes back to a safe situation. Please explain why this strategy usually doesn't work well, and in fact can make the fear worse. Please explain using the concept of reinforcement.

The answer to this starts out with an explanation of what reinforcement is . A reinforcement, or reinforcer, is something that comes after a behavior that makes the behavior more likely to happen again. It's very similar to a reward. Often a reinforcer makes the person feel better than they did before. So the brain learns to do the behavior again, in order to feel better.

What's the idea that this explanation has put forward so far?

A. Our brains tend to repeat the behaviors that have resulted in our feeling better than we did before the behavior took place; in other words, reinforcement makes a behavior more likely.
or
B. Relaxing our muscles tends to make us less scared.

223. When the person escapes from a scary situation to a safer one, the fear usually goes way down. The safer situation is very reinforcing, because it makes the person feel much better. The behavior that is reinforced is escaping from the scary situation. Because that behavior has reinforced, the person will have a stronger urge to

do it the next time. But the urge to escape is about the same thing is fear! So the reinforcement of escape makes the fear greater!

On the other hand, if the person stays in the scary situation until the fear has gone down, the reduction in fear has reinforced the exposure to the situation and not the escape from it!

Which would be wiser, if a person is trying to get over a fear?

A. to practice with a situation that is 10 on a scale of 10 scary, with plans to stay in it for just a short time, and leave when it's too unpleasant,
or
B. to practice with a situation that is 3 on a scale of 10 scary, with plans to stay in it until the fear goes down to about 1 on a scale of 0 to 10?

8.4. What's a different way to think?

224. Here's the fourth requirement for Level 8.

When you are given 5 situations with something someone said to themselves about each situation, come up with two other thoughts about each situation that you think might work better.

You remember the 12 thought exercise. This requirement gives you a chance to use those categories to help you generate ways of thinking that help someone to achieve their goals rather than obstruct them.

One of the most useful questions asked by cognitive therapists is, "What might be a different way to think about that situation? Maybe a way that would work better for you?" Doing this exercise gives you practice at generating better forms of self-talk.

Here's an example of what you might be given:

Situation: Someone wants something really strongly for their birthday, and they tell everyone that this is what they want. But when their birthday comes, they don't get that thing.

Thought: Those people are being so bad to me! I can't handle this!

Now you're asked for two thoughts that might work better.

Thought 1: This is not so bad. I've seen pictures on television of kids who didn't have enough to eat and didn't have clean water and had flies on them. I am definitely not in a bad situation.

Thought 2: What can I do? I can be very gracious and thank everyone for what I did get. I can try to have everybody enjoy this occasion. I can figure out a way to work to earn some money to buy the thing I wanted for myself. I think I'll choose all those options.

The person in this example moved from

A. blaming and awfulizing to not awfulizing and listing and choosing?
or
B. getting down on themselves and learning from the experience to celebrating luck and not blaming someone else?

225. Here's another example of what you do in this requirement:

Situation: The first person plays a very mean prank on the second person. The second person is very embarrassed and feels very bad about it.
Thought: The first person thinks, "Ha ha! I got him, and I got him good! Yay for me!"

Your job is to think of two more useful thoughts.

Thought 1: I made someone feel bad; that was selfish of me. I shouldn't have done that.
Thought 2: I want to try to make it up to that person and avoid doing things like this ever again.

In this example the person moved from

A. Awfulizing to listing options and choosing, and celebrating luck.
or
B. Celebrating their own choice to getting down on themselves and goal-setting. (Getting down on oneself can be a useful thought sometimes!)

8.5. Effort-payoff connection, dissatisfaction-effort connection

226. Here's the fifth requirement for Level 8.

Tell what is meant by the phrases "effort-payoff connection" and "dissatisfaction-effort connection." Tell a little story in which someone gives an example of the dissatisfaction-effort connection. Tell two stories in which someone purposely gets more of an effort-payoff connection into their life.

When someone makes an effort, and something good happens as a result, that's the effort-payoff connection. For example, someone studies hard, and they get a good grade. Someone practices for a music performance, and they do well on their performance. Someone is nice to people, and the people like that person. Someone exercises, and they get more physically fit. Someone tries to lose weight, and they succeed at it. Someone invites a friend to do something, and they have a good time. Someone works at a job, and the person gets paid. Someone volunteers at a job, and the person gets the payoff of knowing they made people happier. Someone reads a book, and they either enjoy the book or learn something worthwhile. Someone discusses a problem with another person, and they make things better by doing so. Someone goes to bed earlier, and they can get up earlier in the morning.

What might someone say to themselves when the OPPOSITE of the effort-payoff connection is present?

A. I worked and I made progress, but it was slow.
or
B. There's no point in doing anything; it's just going to come out bad no matter what.

227. The effort-payoff connection partly depends on our environment. For example, if someone is in a math class that is way, way too hard for that person, it could be that no matter how much effort the person puts out to try to understand this course, there will be only frustration. Or for another example, someone is married to a person who is mean through and through; no matter how much the person tries to help the other person be nice, their efforts are frustrated.

The effort-payoff connection also depends on our own attitude. For example, someone is in a class where it really is possible to do well. But the person thinks, "Oh, what's the use, I'm not going to do well, I might as well not try." There is a possible effort payoff connection in the environment, but not in the person's head. Or someone in a marriage thinks, "It's no use trying to make the relationship better," when they could have succeeded if they had put out the effort.

What's a summary of this?

A. The effort-payoff connection depends on whether it really is possible to make things better, and whether the person thinks it's possible and tries.
or
B. We tend to be happier when there is an effort-payoff connection than when we get the payoffs without effort.

228. People have studied animals kept in captivity, for example in zoos. When the animals don't have to do anything at all, and they are fed at a certain time each day, they do not appear nearly as happy as they do when they have to do something to get their food. This is a piece of evidence that the effort-payoff connection makes animals happier than free payoffs.

Imagine a video game where no matter what you do, you win the game. How much fun would that be? Now imagine one where when you put out lots of effort, you can win. Video games are so addictive because their makers are very good at arranging effort-payoff connections. A video game with free payoffs would not succeed at all.

What's the point of this section?

A. People are happier when they have positive relationships with one another.
or
B. People are generally happier with an effort-payoff connection than they are with free payoffs.

229. The dissatisfaction-effort connection means that when you feel bad about something, you work to make it better. The opposite of this is that you feel bad, so you just withdraw and give up and avoid trying. Here are some examples:

Someone feels worried because there is a big assignment. So the person gets going on it, and sees how much progress is made in a certain time, and calculates how much total time the assignment will take.

Someone doesn't like it that they aren't in shape. So they start exercising.

Someone feels bad about gun violence. So they start researching how to end it, and they write about various solutions.

Someone is annoyed by a habit that a neighbor has. So the person discusses this with the neighbor.

Someone doesn't like it that they don't have any money saved up. So they make a plan and work to earn more and spend less.

Someone feels bad about wasting too much time on Internet entertainment. So the person starts out timing how long they do spend, as a step toward solving this problem.

Which of the following sentences is more connected with the dissatisfaction-effort connection?

A. I saw it, and I was curious about it.
or
B. I didn't like it, so I did something about it.

230. These two connections are very much the opposite of what people often describe as "depression." Often people use the word *depression* to refer to a feeling that "Things are bad, but there's nothing I can do about it." This situation is called learned helplessness. Sentences that go along with this are those such as the following:

Things will never get better.

Why should I even try; I can't succeed.

What's the point of doing anything—it won't make any difference.

I give up.

There's no way out of this.

Suppose something thinks, "I hate the way things are! But I'm going to work really hard to make things better. And I'll count it a victory to know I've done that, even if I don't see results right away!" This person has

A. Learned helplessness,
or
B. A dissatisfaction-effort connection and an effort-payoff connection?

8.6. Strategies for anti-depression

231. Here's the sixth requirement for Level 8.

Suppose that someone wants not to be depressed. Tell several ways that the person can either get over being depressed or avoid getting depressed in the first place.

Here are some ways not to be depressed:

1. Try to have good relationships with people, where people are being nice to each other, helping each other,

solving problems rationally, and caring how things go with each other.

2. Set worthy goals, work toward them, and celebrate every bit of progress.

3. Be aware of what activities you enjoy, and make time for doing those activities.

4. Take the "middle path" regarding work and play, self-indulgence and self-denial: strive for a life where there is work accomplished but there is also fun.

5. Get regular exercise, particularly cardio.

6. Have a consistent sleep rhythm, and get enough sleep.

7. Get enough exposure to bright light, especially in the dark fall and winter.

8. Make good decisions about your self-talk: for example, don't overdo the getting down on yourself and awfulizing and blaming; don't underdo the celebrations.

9. Try to get into situations where there's an effort-payoff connection, and try to arrange your own attitude to maximize the effort-payoff connection. Taking on tasks that are not too hard, not too easy, but just right, promotes the effort-payoff connection.

10. Cultivate the dissatisfaction-effort connection. One form of effort is just talking about the problem and examining it; this is often the first step in making an action plan.

11. Consider acting cheerful or fun-loving or meaningfully engaged with life on purpose, because acting a certain way helps you feel that way too.

12. Avoid environments where you are rewarded for feeling bad.

Do you think the 12 ways of "not being depressed" listed here are also 12 ways of "being more happy?"

A. Yes,
or
B. No?

8.7. What's the point of the lists?

232. Here's the seventh requirement for Level 8.

In this program you have gotten familiar with certain lists. For each of them, tell some (not necessarily all) of the items on the list, and tell how someone could use the concepts in that list to make their life better. In other words, what is the point of getting familiar with this list?

If you are reading this aloud, I recommend that you take turns by paragraph for the rest of this section.

The two big goals: Living a happy life, and helping others to lead happy lives are great goals to have. Thinking about these goals makes it more likely that you'll achieve them.

The sixteen skills and principles (or the 62 skills and principles): These name types of behavior that tend to make life better. If you can look for opportunities to use one of these skills, and celebrate and feel good each time you do so, that in itself can improve the quality of life immensely.

The ten methods of influence (OH RAM PRISM): These are the reasons why people do what they do. If you want to help yourself to behave more in a certain way, you can use these. You can also use them to help other people act in ways that make them and yourself more happy.

The four ways of listening (reflections, facilitations, follow-up questions, positive feedback): When someone talks, and you respond in these ways, it usually helps the person enjoy talking with you, and feel more comfortable with you in general.

Criteria for joint decision-making (Dr. L.W. Aap): If people do these things when they have a conflict with each other or a joint decision to make, they are more likely to work out a good solution and to avoid hostility and violence.

The twelve thoughts: These are 12 different options for how to do self-talk about any situation. If you're able to choose among these and pick the most useful ones for any situation you're in, that will greatly assist you, because self-talk greatly affects how you feel and what you do.

The four thoughts (not awfulizing, goal-setting, listing and choosing, celebrating your own choice): These are 4 of the 12 thoughts that you can do quickly enough to use them all in real life situations. It's good to cultivate them as a reflex for scary or aversive situations and provocations.

Steps in individual decision-making (SOIL ADDLE): Life is a succession of choice points. The better are your decisions, the better your life will be. These are steps that will help you make better decisions.

Ways of responding to provocation (Ida Craft): This list helps you think of different ways of responding to situations that might make someone angry. If people chose wisely among these, the amount of violence and cruelty in the world would be far less!

Ways of reducing anxiety and aversion (Estimating the danger, hierarchy, prolonged exposure (practice), relaxation, self-talk, mental imagery, fantasy rehearsal, skill-building, doing and not feeling to define success): A great deal of unhappiness results from having more fear or other bad feelings attached to certain situations than we need. These methods allow us to reduce the bad feelings that certain situations bring on.

Feeling words: It's good to be able to put words on how you, or someone else, is feeling. This is often the first step in handling a situation well, and figuring out what to do.

Responding to Criticism (T PAARISEC): Handling criticism is very difficult for very many people. This is a list of ways to handle criticism that contributes to good anger control skills and good relations with people.

Ways of relaxing (Relaxing muscles, breathe and relax, mantra, pleasant imagery, loving kindness meditation, kindness to self and others meditation, mind-watching, movement, pleasant dreams, biofeedback, simple rest): For anger control, anxiety reduction, and stress management, it helps to be able to lower your level of arousal, to calm yourself. These are ways that you can practice and use that skill.

Things that people talk about (PAPER): This list helps you think of what to talk about or ask about in conversations.

Contributors to a bad emotional climate (too much of CCCT—commands, criticisms, contradictions, and threats): This is a list of types of utterance that many people could benefit from cutting down on. When these are overdone, the emotional climate suffers.

233. Let's practice connecting up some of these lists with situations where people might use them.

Someone is in the habit of responding to most situations by blaming someone else. The person wants to expand the number of thoughts that pop into their head to use in situations. Which set of ideas would be more useful?

A. The ways of relaxing,
or
B. The twelve thoughts?

234. The person has a disagreement with someone else. The person wants to have a civilized conversation. Which is more useful?

A. Dr. L.W. Aap,
or
B. PAPER?

235. The person is tense and nervous too much of the time. Which is more useful?

A. CCCT,
or
B. The ways of relaxing?

236. The person is facing some important decisions. Which is more useful?

A. SOIL ADDLE,
or
B. OH RAM PRISM?

237. The person wants very much to change their own behavior, for example by giving up alcohol, and they are looking for all the possible ways of helping themselves do that. Which is more useful?

A. T PAARISEC,

or
B. OH RAM PRISM?

238. The person is in a social conversation, and they want to make it pleasant for the other person to talk with them.

A. Four ways of listening,
or
B. Four thought exercise?

www.ingramcontent.com/pod-product-compliance
Lightning Source LLC
LaVergne TN
LVHW010055110826
845155LV00028B/357